UCP 500
+ e UCP

ICC Uniform Customs and Practice for Documentary Credits
and
Supplement to UCP 500 for electronic presentation (eUCP)
Version 1.0

GW00722596

ICC
The world business organization

The Uniform Customs and Practice for Documentary Credits (UCP) were first published by ICC in 1933. Revised versions were issued in 1951, 1962, 1974, 1983 and 1993.

This edition includes the full text of the 1993 revision, which was adopted by the ICC Executive Board in April 1993 and first published as ICC Publication No. 500 in May 1993. It also includes for the first time the Supplement to UCP 500 for Electronic Presentation (eUCP).

This English language edition is the official text. Translations in other languages and bilingual versions may be available from ICC national committees.

Published by

ICC PUBLISHING SA
International Chamber of Commerce
The world business organization
38 Cours Albert 1er
75008 Paris, France

The Uniform Customs and Practice for Documentary Credits (UCP)
first published in May 1993 .
Reprinted in October 1993, January 1994, October 1994, June 1995, June 1996, February 1998, June 1999, November 1999 and June 2001.
This updated and expanded version first published in January 2002.
Copyright © 1993
International Chamber of Commerce

Supplement to UCP 500 for Electronic Presentation (eUCP)
first published in January 2002
Copyright © 2002
International Chamber of Commerce

Reprinted in February 2002, January 2002 and October 2004

ICC Publication No. 500/2
ISBN 92 842 1155 7

FOREWORD

The Foreword to the 1993 revision of UCP 500, ICC's universally used rules on documentary credits, asserted the following: "In a world of fast-changing technology and rapidly improving communications, periodic revision of ICC rules for trade facilitation is inevitable." In fact, the drafters of UCP have always embraced emerging developments in trade: the 1974 revision was drafted in part because of changes in container and combined transport; the 1983 revision responded to new technical standards in transport and telecommunications; and in 1993 UCP 500 took account of "documents produced or appearing to be produced by reprographic, automated or computerized systems", "facsimile signatures" and "electronic methods of communication".

Now, eight years after UCP 500 came into force, ICC has once again anticipated market developments by creating a supplement to UCP that explicitly deals with the electronic presentation of documents. This new supplement, called the UCP Supplement for Electronic Presentation (or eUCP, for short), recognizes that while electronic documents are not yet widely used, they represent a rapidly growing presence in the market. Consequently, a new framework of rules is required to encompass them.

This is the first time that ICC has published a supplement to the UCP. It is important to note that this supplement is an update rather than a full revision of the rules. It is, as the Introduction says, "a bridge between the current UCP and the processing of the electronic equivalent of paper-based credits", and it is to be used in tandem with, not as a replacement for, UCP 500. The authors have wisely concluded that for some time at least, paper documents and electronic documents will co-exist. And the eUCP explicitly caters to part-paper, part-electronic, as well as to all-electronic presentations.

Because UCP and eUCP will work together, the current volume includes the text of both sets of rules, as well as important ICC Banking Commission documents that have been approved since UCP 500 came into force and some key Opinions of the Commission that interpret controversial Articles of the UCP. This combined text serves, not only to introduce the eUCP, but to provide an overview of Banking Commission work.

3

Profound thanks are due to the working group who drafted the original text of the eUCP as well as to the many ICC national committees and individuals who commented on and improved the various drafts. This combined effort has produced a set of rules which, like UCP, will serve as a benchmark in their field.

Maria Livanos Cattaui
Secretary General
International Chamber of Commerce
Paris, France
December 2001

CONTENTS

The title or classification on the heading of each Article is for reference as to intent and purpose. It is not to be construed as being other than solely for the benefit or guidance and there should be no legal imputation.

ICC Uniform Customs & Practice for Documentary Credits

Supplement to UCP 500 for Electronic Presentation (eUCP)

ICC Banking Commission Decisions & Policy Statements

Selected Opinions of the ICC Banking Commission

ICC Uniform Customs and Practice for

Documentary Credits

UCP 500

1993 revision in force as of 1 January 1994

Adopted by UNCITRAL on 13 July 1994

A. GENERAL PROVISIONS AND DEFINITIONS

Article 1

Application of UCP

The Uniform Customs and Practice for Documentary Credits, 1993 Revision, ICC Publication No. 500, shall apply to all Documentary Credits (including to the extent to which they may be applicable, Standby Letter(s) of Credit) where they are incorporated into the text of the Credit. They are binding on all parties thereto, unless otherwise expressly stipulated in the Credit.

Article 2

Meaning of Credit

For the purposes of these Articles, the expressions "Documentary Credit(s)" and "Standby Letter(s) of Credit" (hereinafter referred to as "Credit(s)"), mean any arrangement, however named or described, whereby a bank (the "Issuing Bank") acting at the request and on the instructions of a customer (the "Applicant") or on its own behalf,

   i. is to make a payment to or to the order of a third party (the"Beneficiary"), or is to accept and pay bills of exchange (Draft(s)) drawn by the Beneficiary,

     or

   ii. authorises another bank to effect such payment, or to accept and pay such bills of exchange (Draft(s)),

     or

   iii. authorises another bank to negotiate,

against stipulated document(s),provided that the terms and conditions of the Credit are complied with.

For the purposes of these Articles, branches of a bank in different countries are considered another bank.

Article 3

Credits v. Contracts

a Credits, by their nature, are separate transactions from the sales or other contract(s) on which they may be based and banks are in no way concerned with or bound by such contract(s), even if any reference whatsoever to such contract(s) is included in the Credit. Consequently, the undertaking of a bank to pay, accept and pay Draft(s) or negotiate and/or to fulfil any other obligation under the Credit, is not subject to claims or defences by the Applicant resulting from his relationships with the Issuing Bank or the Beneficiary.

b A Beneficiary can in no case avail himself of the contractual relationships existing between the banks or between the Applicant and the Issuing Bank.

Article 4

Documents v. Goods/Services/Performances

In Credit operations all parties concerned deal with documents, and not with goods, services and/or other performances to which the documents may relate.

Article 5

Instructions to Issue/Amend Credits

a Instructions for the issuance of a Credit, the Credit itself, instructions for an amendment thereto, and the amendment itself, must be complete and precise.

In order to guard against confusion and misunderstanding, banks should discourage any attempt:

i. to include excessive detail in the Credit or in any amendment thereto;

ii. to give instructions to issue, advise or confirm a Credit by reference to a Credit previously issued (similar Credit) where such previous Credit has been subject to accepted amendment(s), and/or unaccepted amendment(s).

b   All instructions for the issuance of a Credit and the Credit itself and, where applicable, all instructions for an amendment thereto and the amendment itself, must state precisely the document(s) against which payment, acceptance or negotiation is to be made.

B. FORM AND NOTIFICATION OF CREDITS

Article 6

Revocable v. Irrevocable Credits

a   A Credit may be either

   i.   revocable,

      or

   ii.   irrevocable.

b   The Credit, therefore, should clearly indicate whether it is revocable or irrevocable.

c   In the absence of such indication the Credit shall be deemed to be irrevocable.

Article 7

Advising Bank's Liability

a   A Credit may be advised to a Beneficiary through another bank (the "Advising Bank") without engage-ment on the part of the Advising Bank, but that bank, if it elects to advise the Credit, shall take reasonable care to check the apparent authenticity of the Credit which it advises. If the bank elects not to advise the Credit, it must so inform the Issuing Bank without delay.

b   If the Advising Bank cannot establish such apparent authenticity it must inform, without delay, the bank from which the instructions appear to have been received that it has been unable to establish the authenticity of the Credit and if it elects nonetheless to advise the Credit it must inform the Beneficiary that it has not been able to establish the authenticity of the Credit.

Article 8

Revocation of a Credit

a A revocable Credit may be amended or cancelled by the Issuing Bank at any moment and without prior notice to the Beneficiary.

b However, the Issuing Bank must:

i. reimburse another bank with which a revocable Credit has been made available for sight payment, acceptance or negotiation – for any payment, acceptance or negotiation made by such bank – prior to receipt by it of notice of amendment or cancellation, against documents which appear on their face to be in compliance with the terms and conditions of the Credit;

ii. reimburse another bank with which a revocable Credit has been made available for deferred payment, if such a bank has, prior to receipt by it of notice of amendment or cancellation, taken up documents which appear on their face to be in compliance with the terms and conditions of the Credit.

Article 9

Liability of Issuing and Confirming Banks

a An irrevocable Credit constitutes a definite undertaking of the Issuing Bank, provided that the stipulated documents are presented to the Nominated Bank or to the Issuing Bank and that the terms and conditions of the Credit are complied with:

i. if the Credit provides for sight payment – to pay at sight;

ii. if the Credit provides for deferred payment – to pay on the maturity date(s) determinable in accordance with the stipulations of the Credit;

iii. if the Credit provides for acceptance:

a) by the Issuing Bank – to accept Draft(s) drawn by the Beneficiary on the Issuing Bank and pay them at maturity,

or

b) by another drawee bank – to accept and pay at maturity Draft(s) drawn by the Beneficiary on the Issuing Bank in the event the drawee bank stipulated in the Credit does not accept Draft(s) drawn on it, or to pay Draft(s) accepted but not paid by such drawee bank at maturity;

iv. if the Credit provides for negotiation – to pay without recourse to drawers and/or bona fide holders, Draft(s) drawn by the Beneficiary and/or document(s) presented under the Credit. A Credit should not be issued available by Draft(s) on the Applicant. If the Credit nevertheless calls for Draft(s) on the Applicant, banks will consider such Draft(s) as an additional document(s).

b A confirmation of an irrevocable Credit by another bank (the "Confirming Bank") upon the authorisation or request of the Issuing Bank, constitutes a definite undertaking of the Confirming Bank, in addition to that of the Issuing Bank, provided that the stipulated documents are presented to the Confirming Bank or to any other Nominated Bank and that the terms and conditions of the Credit are complied with:

i. if the Credit provides for sight payment – to pay at sight;

ii. if the Credit provides for deferred payment – to pay on the maturity date(s) determinable in accordance with the stipulations of the Credit;

iii. if the Credit provides for acceptance:

a) by the Confirming Bank – to accept Draft(s) drawn by the Beneficiary on the Confirming Bank and pay them at maturity,

or

b) by another drawee bank – to accept and pay at maturity Draft(s) drawn by the Beneficiary on the Confirming Bank, in the event the drawee bank stipulated in the Credit does not accept Draft(s) drawn on it, or to pay Draft(s) accepted but not paid by such drawee bank at maturity;

iv. if the Credit provides for negotiation – to negotiate without recourse to drawers and/or bona fide holders, Draft(s) drawn by the Beneficiary and/or document(s) presented under the Credit. A Credit should not be issued available by Draft(s) on the Applicant. If the Credit nevertheless calls for Draft(s) on the Applicant, banks will consider such Draft(s) as an additional document(s).

c **i.** If another bank is authorised or requested by the Issuing Bank to add its confirmation to a Credit but is not prepared to do so, it must so inform the Issuing Bank without delay.

ii. Unless the Issuing Bank specifies otherwise in its authorisation or request to add confirmation, the Advising Bank may advise the Credit to the Beneficiary without adding its confirmation.

d **i.** Except as otherwise provided by Article 48, an irrevocable Credit can neither be amended nor cancelled without the agreement of the Issuing Bank, the Confirming Bank, if any, and the Beneficiary.

ii. The Issuing Bank shall be irrevocably bound by an amendment(s) issued by it from the time of the issuance of such amendment(s). A Confirming Bank may extend its confirmation to an amendment and shall be irrevocably bound as of the time of its advice of the amendment. A Confirming Bank may, however, choose to advise an amendment to the Beneficiary without extending its confirmation and if so, must inform the Issuing Bank and the Beneficiary without delay.

iii. The terms of the original Credit (or a Credit incorporating previously accepted amend-ment(s)) will remain in force for the Beneficiary until the Beneficiary communicates his acceptance of the amendment to the bank that advised such amendment. The Beneficiary should give notification of acceptance or rejection of amendment(s). If the Beneficiary fails to give such notification, the tender of documents to the Nominated Bank or Issuing Bank, that conform to the Credit and to not yet accepted amendment(s), will be deemed to be notification of acceptance by the Beneficiary of such amendment(s) and as of that moment the Credit will be amended.

iv. Partial acceptance of amendments contained in one and the same advice of amendment is not allowed and consequently will not be given any effect.

Article 10

Types of Credit

a All Credits must clearly indicate whether they are available by sight payment, by deferred payment, by acceptance or by negotiation.

b **i.** Unless the Credit stipulates that it is available only with the Issuing Bank, all Credits must nominate the bank (the "Nominated Bank") which is authorised to pay, to incur a deferred payment undertaking, to accept Draft(s) or to negotiate. In a freely negotiable Credit, any bank is a Nominated Bank.

Presentation of documents must be made to the Issuing Bank or the Confirming Bank, if any, or any other Nominated Bank.

ii. Negotiation means the giving of value for Draft(s) and/or document(s) by the bank authorised to negotiate. Mere examination of the documents without giving of value does not constitute a negotiation.

c Unless the Nominated Bank is the Confirming Bank, nomination by the Issuing Bank does not constitute any undertaking by the Nominated Bank to pay, to incur a deferred payment undertaking, to accept Draft(s), or to negotiate. Except where expressly agreed to by the Nominated Bank and so communicated to the Beneficiary, the Nominated Bank's receipt of and/or examination and/or forwarding of the documents does not make that bank liable to pay, to incur a deferred payment undertaking, to accept Draft(s), or to negotiate.

d By nominating another bank, or by allowing for negotiation by any bank, or by authorising or requesting another bank to add its confirmation, the Issuing Bank authorises such bank to pay, accept Draft(s) or negotiate as the case may be, against documents which appear on their face to be in compliance with the terms and conditions of the Credit and undertakes to reimburse such bank in accordance with the provisions of these Articles.

Article 11

Teletransmitted and Pre-Advised Credits

a **i.** When an Issuing Bank instructs an Advising Bank by an authenticated teletransmission to advise a Credit or an amendment to a Credit, the teletransmission will be deemed to be the operative Credit instrument or the operative amendment, and no mail confirmation should be sent. Should a mail confirmation nevertheless be sent, it will have no effect and the Advising Bank will have no obligation to check such mail confirmation against the operative Credit instrument or the operative Credit instrument or the operative amendment received by teletransmission.

ii. If the teletransmission states "full details to follow" (or words of similar effect) or states that the mail confirmation is to be the operative Credit instrument or the operative amendment, then the teletransmission will not be deemed to be the operative Credit instrument or the operative amendment. The Issuing Bank must forward the operative Credit instrument or the operative amendment to such Advising Bank without delay.

b If a bank uses the services of an Advising Bank to have the Credit advised to the Beneficiary, it must also use the services of the same bank for advising an amendment(s).

c A preliminary advice of the issuance or amendment of an irrevocable Credit (pre-advice), shall only be given by an Issuing Bank if such bank is prepared to issue the operative Credit instrument or the operative amendment thereto. Unless otherwise stated in such preliminary advice by the Issuing Bank, an Issuing Bank having given such pre-advice shall be irrevocably committed to issue or amend the Credit, in terms not inconsistent with the pre-advice, without delay.

Article 12

Incomplete or Unclear Instructions

If incomplete or unclear instructions are received to advise, confirm or amend a Credit, the bank requested to act on such instructions may give preliminary notification to the Beneficiary for information only and without responsibility. This preliminary notification should state clearly that the notification is provided for information only and without the responsibility of the Advising Bank. In any event, the Advising Bank must inform the Issuing Bank of the action taken and request it to provide the necessary information.

The Issuing Bank must provide the necessary information without delay. The Credit will be advised, confirmed or amended, only when complete and clear instructions have been received and if the Advising Bank is then prepared to act on the instructions.

C. LIABILITIES AND RESPONSIBILITIES

Article 13

Standard for Examination of Documents

a   Banks must examine all documents stipulated in the Credit with reasonable care, to ascertain whether or not they appear, on their face, to be in compliance with the terms and conditions of the Credit. Compliance of the stipulated documents on their face with the terms and conditions of the Credit, shall be determined by international standard banking practice as reflected in these Articles. Documents which appear on their face to be inconsistent with one another will be considered as not appearing on their face to be in compliance with the terms and conditions of the Credit.

Documents not stipulated in the Credit will not be examined by banks. If they receive such documents, they shall return them to the presenter or pass them on without responsibility.

b   The Issuing Bank, the Confirming Bank, if any, or a Nominated Bank acting on their behalf, shall each have a reasonable time, not to exceed seven banking days following the day of receipt of the documents, to examine the documents and determine whether to take up or refuse the documents and to inform the party from which it received the documents accordingly.

c   If a Credit contains conditions without stating the document(s) to be presented in compliance therewith, banks will deem such conditions as not stated and will disregard them.

Article 14

Discrepant Documents and Notice

a   When the Issuing Bank authorises another bank to pay, incur a deferred payment undertaking, accept Draft(s), or negotiate against documents which appear on their face to be in compliance with the terms and conditions of the Credit, the Issuing Bank and the Confirming Bank, if any, are bound:

    i.   to reimburse the Nominated Bank which has paid, incurred a deferred payment undertaking, accepted Draft(s), or negotiated,

ii. to take up the documents.

b Upon receipt of the documents the Issuing Bank and/or Confirming Bank, if any, or a Nominated Bank acting on their behalf, must determine on the basis of the documents alone whether or not they appear on their face to be in compliance with the terms and conditions of the Credit. If the documents appear on their face not to be in compliance with the terms and conditions of the Credit, such banks may refuse to take up the documents.

c If the Issuing Bank determines that the documents appear on their face not to be in compliance with the terms and conditions of the Credit, it may in its sole judgment approach the Applicant for a waiver of the discrepancy(ies). This does not, however, extend the period mentioned in sub-Article 13 (b).

d **i.** If the Issuing Bank and/or Confirming Bank, if any, or a Nominated Bank acting on their behalf, decides to refuse the documents, it must give notice to that effect by tele-communication or, if that is not possible, by other expeditious means, without delay but no later than the close of the seventh banking day following the day of receipt of the documents. Such notice shall be given to the bank from which it received the documents, or to the Beneficiary, if it received the documents directly from him.

ii. Such notice must state all discrepancies in respect of which the bank refuses the documents and must also state whether it is holding the documents at the disposal of, or is returning them to, the presenter.

iii. The Issuing Bank and/or Confirming Bank, if any, shall then be entitled to claim from the remitting bank refund, with interest, of any reimbursement which has been made to that bank.

e If the Issuing Bank and/or Confirming Bank, if any, fails to act in accordance with the provisions of this Article and/or fails to hold the documents at the disposal of, or return them to the presenter, the Issuing Bank and/or Confirming Bank, if any, shall be precluded from claiming that the documents are not in compliance with the terms and conditions of the Credit.

f If the remitting bank draws the attention of the Issuing Bank and/or Confirming Bank, if any, to any discrepancy(ies) in the document(s) or advises such banks that it has paid, incurred a deferred payment undertaking, accepted Draft(s) or negotiated under reserve or against an indemnity in respect of such discrepancy(ies), the Issuing Bank and/or Confirming Bank, if any, shall not be thereby relieved from any of their obligations under any provision of this Article. Such reserve or indemnity concerns only the relations between the remitting bank and the party towards whom the reserve was made, or from whom, or on whose behalf, the indemnity was obtained.

Article 15

Disclaimer on Effectiveness of Documents

Banks assume no liability or responsibility for the form, sufficiency, accuracy, genuineness, falsification or legal effect of any document(s), or for the general and/or particular conditions stipulated in the document(s) or superimposed thereon; nor do they assume any liability or responsibility for the description, quantity, weight, quality, condition, packing, delivery, value or existence of the goods represented by any document(s), or for the good faith or acts and/or omissions, solvency, performance or standing of the consignors, the carriers, the forwarders, the consignees or the insurers of the goods, or any other person whomsoever.

Article 16

Disclaimer on the Transmission of Messages

Banks assume no liability or responsibility for the consequences arising out of delay and/or loss in transit of any message(s), letter(s) or document(s), or for delay, mutilation or other error(s) arising in the transmission of any telecommunication. Banks assume no liability or responsibility for errors in translation and/or interpretation of technical terms, and reserve the right to transmit Credit terms without translating them.

Article 17

Force Majeure

Banks assume no liability or responsibility for the consequences arising out of the interruption of their business by Acts of God, riots, civil commotions, insurrections, wars or any other causes beyond their control, or by any strikes or lockouts. Unless specifically authorised, banks will not, upon resumption of their business, pay, incur a deferred payment undertaking, accept Draft(s) or negotiate under Credits which expired during such interruption of their business.

Article 18

Disclaimer for Acts of an Instructed Party

a Banks utilizing the services of another bank or other banks for the purpose of giving effect to the instructions of the Applicant do so for the account and at the risk of such Applicant.

b Banks assume no liability or responsibility should the instructions they transmit not be carried out, even if they have themselves taken the initiative in the choice of such other bank(s).

c **i.** A party instructing another party to perform services is liable for any charges, including commissions, fees, costs or expenses incurred by the instructed party in connection with its instructions.

    ii. Where a Credit stipulates that such charges are for the account of a party other than the instructing party, and charges cannot be collected, the instructing party remains ultimately liable for the payment thereof.

d The Applicant shall be bound by and liable to indemnify the banks against all obligations and responsibilities imposed by foreign laws and usages.

Article 19

Bank-to-Bank Reimbursement Arrangements

a   If an Issuing Bank intends that the reimbursement to which a paying, accepting or negotiating bank is entitled, shall be obtained by such bank (the "Claiming Bank"), claiming on another party (the "Reimbursing Bank"), it shall provide such Reimbursing Bank in good time with the proper instructions or authorisation to honour such reimbursement claims.

b   Issuing Banks shall not require a Claiming Bank to supply a certificate of compliance with the terms and conditions of the Credit to the Reimbursing Bank.

c   An Issuing Bank shall not be relieved from any of its obligations to provide reimbursement if and when reimbursement is not received by the Claiming Bank from the Reimbursing Bank.

d   The Issuing Bank shall be responsible to the Claiming Bank for any loss of interest if reimbursement is not provided by the Reimbursing Bank on first demand, or as otherwise specified in the Credit, or mutually agreed, as the case may be.

e   The Reimbursing Bank's charges should be for the account of the Issuing Bank. However, in cases where the charges are for the account of another party, it is the responsibility of the Issuing Bank to so indicate in the original Credit and in the reimbursement authorisation. In cases where the Reimbursing Bank's charges are for the account of another party they shall be collected from the Claiming Bank when the Credit is drawn under. In cases where the Credit is not drawn under, the Reimbursing Bank's charges remain the obligation of the Issuing Bank.

D. DOCUMENTS

Article 20

Ambiguity as to the Issuers of Documents

a   Terms such as "first class", "well known", "qualified", "independent", "official", "competent", "local" and the like, shall not be used to describe the issuers of any document(s) to be presented under a Credit. If such terms are incorporated in the Credit, banks will accept the relative document(s) as presented, provided that it appears on its face to be in compliance with the other terms and conditions of the Credit and not to have been issued by the Beneficiary.

b   Unless otherwise stipulated in the Credit, banks will also accept as an original document(s), a document(s) produced or appearing to have been produced:

     i.   by reprographic, automated or computerized systems;

     ii.   as carbon copies;

   provided that it is marked as original and, where necessary, appears to be signed.

   A document may be signed by handwriting, by facsimile signature, by perforated signature, by stamp, by symbol, or by any other mechanical or electronic method of authentication.

c   **i.**   Unless otherwise stipulated in the Credit, banks will accept as a copy(ies), a document(s) either labelled copy or not marked as an original – a copy(ies) need not be signed.

     ii.   Credits that require multiple document(s) such as "duplicate", "two fold", "two copies" and the like, will be satisfied by the presentation of one original and the remaining number in copies except where the document itself indicates otherwise.

d   Unless otherwise stipulated in the Credit, a condition under a Credit calling for a document to be authenticated, validated, legalised, visaed, certified or indicating a similar requirement, will be satisfied by any signature, mark, stamp or label on such document that on its face appears to satisfy the above condition.

Article 21

Unspecified Issuers or Contents of Documents

When documents other than transport documents, insurance documents and commercial invoices are called for, the Credit should stipulate by whom such documents are to be issued and their wording or data content. If the Credit does not so stipulate, banks will accept such documents as presented, provided that their data content is not inconsistent with any other stipulated document presented.

Article 22

Issuance Date of Documents v. Credit Date

Unless otherwise stipulated in the Credit, banks will accept a document bearing a date of issuance prior to that of the Credit, subject to such document being presented within the time limits set out in the Credit and in these Articles.

Article 23

Marine/Ocean Bill of Lading

a   If a Credit calls for a bill of lading covering a port-to-port shipment, banks will, unless otherwise stipulated in the Credit, accept a document, however named, which:

    i.   appears on its face to indicate the name of the carrier and to have been signed or otherwise authenticated by:

       –   the carrier or a named agent for or on behalf of the carrier, or

       –   the master or a named agent for or on behalf of the master.

       Any signature or authentication of the carrier or master must be identified as carrier or master, as the case may be. An agent signing or authenticating for the carrier or master must also indicate the name and the capacity of the party, i.e. carrier or master, on whose behalf that agent is acting,

       and

    ii.   indicates that the goods have been loaded on board, or shipped on a named vessel.

Loading on board or shipment on a named vessel may be indicated by pre-printed wording on the bill of lading that the goods have been loaded on board a named vessel or shipped on a named vessel, in which case the date of issuance of the bill of lading will be deemed to be the date of loading on board and the date of shipment.

In all other cases loading on board a named vessel must be evidenced by a notation on the bill of lading which gives the date on which the goods have been loaded on board, in which case the date of the on board notation will be deemed to be the date of shipment.

If the bill of lading contains the indication "intended vessel", or similar qualification in relation to the vessel, loading on board a named vessel must be evidenced by an on board notation on the bill of lading which, in addition to the date on which the goods have been loaded on board, also includes the name of the vessel on which the goods have been loaded, even if they have been loaded on the vessel named as the "intended vessel".

If the bill of lading indicates a place of receipt or taking in charge different from the port of loading, the on board notation must also include the port of loading stipulated in the Credit and the name of the vessel on which the goods have been loaded, even if they have been loaded on the vessel named in the bill of lading. This provision also applies whenever loading on board the vessel is indicated by pre-printed wording on the bill of lading,

and

iii. indicates the port of loading and the port of discharge stipulated in the Credit, notwithstand-ing that it:

   a) indicates a place of taking in charge different from the port of loading, and/or a place of final destination different from the port of discharge,

   and/or

   b) contains the indication "intended" or similar qualification in relation to the port of loading and/or port of discharge, as long as the document also states the ports of loading and/or discharge stipulated in the Credit,

   and

iv. consists of a sole original bill of lading or, if issued in more than one original, the full set as so issued,

and

v. appears to contain all of the terms and conditions of carriage, or some of such terms and conditions by reference to a source or document other than the bill of lading (short form/blank back bill of lading); banks will not examine the contents of such terms and conditions,

and

vi. contains no indication that it is subject to a charter party and/ or no indication that the carrying vessel is propelled by sail only,

and

vii. in all other respects meets the stipulations of the Credit.

b For the purpose of this Article, transhipment means unloading and reloading from one vessel to another vessel during the course of ocean carriage from the port of loading to the port of discharge stipulated in the Credit.

c Unless transhipment is prohibited by the terms of the Credit, banks will accept a bill of lading which indicates that the goods will be transhipped, provided that the entire ocean carriage is covered by one and the same bill of lading.

d Even if the Credit prohibits transhipment, banks will accept a bill of lading which:

i. indicates that transhipment will take place as long as the relevant cargo is shipped in Container(s), Trailer(s) and/or "LASH" barge(s) as evidenced by the bill of lading, provided that the entire ocean carriage is covered by one and the same bill of lading,

and/or

ii. incorporates clauses stating that the carrier reserves the right to tranship.

Article 24

Non-Negotiable Sea Waybill

a If a Credit calls for a non-negotiable sea waybill covering a port-to-port shipment, banks will, unless otherwise stipulated in the Credit, accept a document, however named, which:

i. appears on its face to indicate the name of the carrier and to have been signed or otherwise authenticated by:

– the carrier or a named agent for or on behalf of the carrier, or

– the master or a named agent for or on behalf of the master,

Any signature or authentication of the carrier or master must be identified as carrier or master, as the case may be. An agent signing or authenticating for the carrier or master must also indicate the name and the capacity of the party, i.e. carrier or master, on whose behalf that agent is acting,

and

ii. indicates that the goods have been loaded on board, or shipped on a named vessel.

Loading on board or shipment on a named vessel may be indicated by pre-printed wording on the non-negotiable sea waybill that the goods have been loaded on board a named vessel or shipped on a named vessel, in which case the date of issuance of the non-negotiable sea waybill will be deemed to be the date of loading on board and the date of shipment.

In all other cases loading on board a named vessel must be evidenced by a notation on the non-negotiable sea waybill which gives the date on which the goods have been loaded on board, in which case the date of the on board notation will be deemed to be the date of shipment.

If the non-negotiable sea waybill contains the indication "intended vessel", or similar qualification in relation to the vessel, loading on board a named vessel must be evidenced by an on board notation on the non-negotiable sea waybill which, in addition to the date on which the goods have been loaded on board, includes the name of the vessel on which the goods have been loaded, even if they have been loaded on the vessel named as the "intended vessel".

If the non-negotiable sea waybill indicates a place of receipt or taking in charge different from the port of loading, the on board notation must also include the port of loading stipulated in the Credit and the name of the vessel on which the goods have been loaded, even if they have been loaded on a vessel named in the non-negotiable sea waybill. This provision also applies whenever loading on board the vessel is indicated by pre-printed wording on the non-negotiable sea waybill,

and

iii. indicates the port of loading and the port of discharge stipulated in the Credit, notwithstand-ing that it:

a) indicates a place of taking in charge different from the port of loading, and/or a place of final destination different from the port of discharge,

and/or

b) contains the indication "intended" or similar qualification in relation to the port of loading and/or port of discharge, as long as the document also states the ports of loading and/or discharge stipulated in the Credit,

and

iv. consists of a sole original non-negotiable sea waybill, or if issued in more than one original, the full set as so issued,

and

v. appears to contain all of the terms and conditions of carriage, or some of such terms and conditions by reference to a source or document other than the non-negotiable sea waybill (short form/blank back non-negotiable sea waybill); banks will not examine the contents of such terms and conditions,

and

vi. contains no indication that it is subject to a charter party and/or no indication that the carrying vessel is propelled by sail only,

and

vii. in all other respects meets the stipulations of the Credit.

b   For the purpose of this Article, transhipment means unloading and reloading from one vessel to another vessel during the course of ocean carriage from the port of loading to the port of discharge stipulated in the Credit.

c   Unless transhipment is prohibited by the terms of the Credit, banks will accept a non-negotiable sea waybill which indicates that the goods will be transhipped, provided that the entire ocean carriage is covered by one and the same non-negotiable sea waybill.

d   Even if the Credit prohibits transhipment, banks will accept a non-negotiable sea waybill which:

   i.   indicates that transhipment will take place as long as the relevant cargo is shipped in Container(s), Trailer(s) and/or "LASH" barge(s) as evidenced by the non-negotiable sea waybill, provided that the entire ocean carriage is covered by one and the same non-negotiable sea waybill,

   and/or

   ii.   incorporates clauses stating that the carrier reserves the right to tranship.

Article 25

Charter Party Bill of Lading

a   If a Credit calls for or permits a charter party bill of lading, banks will, unless otherwise stipulated in the Credit, accept a document, however named, which:

   i.   contains any indication that it is subject to a charter party,

   and

   ii.   appears on its face to have been signed or otherwise authenticated by:

   —   the master or a named agent for or on behalf of the master, or

   —   the owner or a named agent for or on behalf of the owner.

   Any signature or authentication of the master or owner must be identified as master or owner as the case may be. An agent signing or authen-ticating for the master or owner must also indicate the name and the capacity of the party, i.e. master or owner, on whose behalf that agent is acting,

and

iii. does or does not indicate the name of the carrier,

and

iv. indicates that the goods have been loaded on board or shipped on a named vessel.

Loading on board or shipment on a named vessel may be indicated by pre-printed wording on the bill of lading that the goods have been loaded on board a named vessel or shipped on a named vessel, in which case the date of issuance of the bill of lading will be deemed to be the date of loading on board and the date of shipment.

In all other cases loading on board a named vessel must be evidenced by a notation on the bill of lading which gives the date on which the goods have been loaded on board, in which case the date of the on board notation will be deemed to be the date of shipment,

and

v. indicates the port of loading and the port of discharge stipulated in the Credit,

and

vi. consists of a sole original bill of lading or, if issued in more than one original, the full set as so issued,

and

vii. contains no indication that the carrying vessel is propelled by sail only,

and

viii. in all other respects meets the stipulations of the Credit.

b Even if the Credit requires the presentation of a charter party contract in connection with a charter party bill of lading, banks will not examine such charter party contract, but will pass it on without responsibility on their part.

Article 26

Multimodal Transport Document

a If a Credit calls for a transport document covering at least two different modes of transport (multimodal transport), banks will, unless otherwise stipulated in the Credit, accept a document, however named, which:

   i. appears on its face to indicate the name of the carrier or multimodal transport operator and to have been signed or otherwise authenticated by:

     – the carrier or multimodal transport operator or a named agent for or on behalf of the carrier or multimodal transport operator,

     or

     – the master or a named agent for or on behalf of the master.

     Any signature or authentication of the carrier, multimodal transport operator or master must be identified as carrier, multimodal transport operator or master, as the case may be. An agent signing or authenticating for the carrier, multimodal transport operator or master must also indicate the name and the capacity of the party, i.e. carrier, multimodal transport operator or master, on whose behalf that agent is acting,

     and

   ii. indicates that the goods have been dispatched, taken in charge or loaded on board.

     Dispatch, taking in charge or loading on board may be indicated by wording to that effect on the multimodal transport document and the date of issuance will be deemed to be the date of dispatch, taking in charge or loading on board and the date of shipment. However, if the document indicates, by stamp or otherwise, a date of dispatch, taking in charge or loading on board, such date will be deemed to be the date of shipment,

     and

   iii. **a)** indicates the place of taking in charge stipulated in the Credit which may be different from the port, airport or place of loading, and the place of final destination stipulated in the Credit which may be different from the port, airport or place of discharge, and/or

b) contains the indication "intended" or similar qualification in relation to the vessel and/or port of loading and/or port of discharge,

and

iv. consists of a sole original multimodal transport document or, if issued in more than one original, the full set as so issued,

and

v. appears to contain all of the terms and conditions of carriage, or some of such terms and conditions by reference to a source or document other than the multimodal transport document (short form/blank back multimodal transport document); banks will not examine the contents of such terms and conditions,

and

vi. contains no indication that it is subject to a charter party and/ or no indication that the carrying vessel is propelled by sail only,

and

vii. in all other respects meets the stipulations of the Credit.

b Even if the Credit prohibits transhipment, banks will accept a multimodal transport document which indicates that transhipment will or may take place, provided that the entire carriage is covered by one and the same multimodal transport document.

Article 27

Air Transport Document

a If a Credit calls for an air transport document, banks will, unless otherwise stipulated in the Credit, accept a document, however named, which:

i. appears on its face to indicate the name of the carrier and to have been signed or otherwise authenticated by:

– the carrier, or

– a named agent for or on behalf of the carrier.

Any signature or authentication of the carrier must be identified as carrier. An agent signing or authenticating for the carrier must also indicate the name and the capacity of the party, i.e. carrier, on whose behalf that agent is acting,

and

ii. indicates that the goods have been accepted for carriage,

and

iii. where the Credit calls for an actual date of dispatch, indicates a specific notation of such date, the date of dispatch so indicated on the air transport document will be deemed to be the date of shipment.

For the purpose of this Article, the information appearing in the box on the air transport document (marked "For Carrier Use Only" or similar expression) relative to the flight number and date will not be considered as a specific notation of such date of dispatch.

In all other cases, the date of issuance of the air transport document will be deemed to be the date of shipment,

and

iv. indicates the airport of departure and the airport of destination stipulated in the Credit,

and

v. appears to be the original for consignor/shipper even if the Credit stipulates a full set of originals, or similar expressions,

and

vi. appears to contain all of the terms and conditions of carriage, or some of such terms and conditions, by reference to a source or document other than the air transport document; banks will not examine the contents of such terms and conditions,

and

vii. in all other respects meets the stipulations of the Credit.

b For the purpose of this Article, transhipment means unloading and reloading from one aircraft to another aircraft during the course of carriage from the airport of departure to the airport of destination stipulated in the Credit.

c Even if the Credit prohibits transhipment, banks will accept an air transport document which indicates that transhipment will or may take place, provided that the entire carriage is covered by one and the same air transport document.

Article 28

Road, Rail or Inland Waterway Transport Documents

a If a Credit calls for a road, rail, or inland waterway transport document, banks will, unless otherwise stipulated in the Credit, accept a document of the type called for, however named, which:

i. appears on its face to indicate the name of the carrier and to have been signed or otherwise authenticated by the carrier or a named agent for or on behalf of the carrier and/or to bear a reception stamp or other indication of receipt by the carrier or a named agent for or on behalf of the carrier.

Any signature, authentication, reception stamp or other indication of receipt of the carrier, must be identified on its face as that of the carrier. An agent signing or authenticating for the carrier, must also indicate the name and the capacity of the party, i.e. carrier, on whose behalf that agent is acting,

and

ii. indicates that the goods have been received for shipment, dispatch or carriage or wording to this effect. The date of issuance will be deemed to be the date of shipment unless the transport document contains a reception stamp, in which case the date of the reception stamp will be deemed to be the date of shipment,

and

iii. indicates the place of shipment and the place of destination stipulated in the Credit,

and

iv. in all other respects meets the stipulations of the Credit.

b   In the absence of any indication on the transport document as to the numbers issued, banks will accept the transport document(s) presented as constituting a full set. Banks will accept as original(s) the transport document(s) whether marked as original(s) or not.

c   For the purpose of this Article, transhipment means unloading and reloading from one means of conveyance to another means of conveyance, in different modes of transport, during the course of carriage from the place of shipment to the place of destination stipulated in the Credit.

d   Even if the Credit prohibits transhipment, banks will accept a road, rail, or inland waterway transport document which indicates that transhipment will or may take place, provided that the entire carriage is covered by one and the same transport document and within the same mode of transport.

Article 29

Courier and Post Receipts

a   If a Credit calls for a post receipt or certificate of posting, banks will, unless otherwise stipulated in the Credit, accept a post receipt or certificate of posting which:

i.   appears on its face to have been stamped or otherwise authenticated and dated in the place from which the Credit stipulates the goods are to be shipped or dispatched and such date will be deemed to be the date of shipment or dispatch,

and

ii.   in all other respects meets the stipulations of the Credit.

b   If a Credit calls for a document issued by a courier or expedited delivery service evidencing receipt of the goods for delivery, banks will, unless otherwise stipulated in the Credit, accept a document, however named, which:

i.   appears on its face to indicate the name of the courier/service, and to have been stamped, signed or otherwise authenticated by such named courier/service (unless the Credit specifically calls for a document issued by a named Courier/Service, banks will accept a document issued by any Courier/Service),

and

ii.   indicates a date of pick-up or of receipt or wording to this effect, such date being deemed to be the date of shipment or dispatch,

and

iii. in all other respects meets the stipulations of the Credit.

Article 30

Transport Documents issued by Freight Forwarders

Unless otherwise authorised in the Credit, banks will only accept a transport document issued by a freight forwarder if it appears on its face to indicate:

i.   the name of the freight forwarder as a carrier or multimodal transport operator and to have been signed or otherwise authenticated by the freight forwarder as carrier or multimodal transport operator,

or

ii. the name of the carrier or multimodal transport operator and to have been signed or otherwise authenticated by the freight forwarder as a named agent for or on behalf of the carrier or multimodal transport operator.

Article 31

"On Deck", "Shipper's Load and Count", Name of Consignor

Unless otherwise stipulated in the Credit, banks will accept a transport document which:

i.   does not indicate, in the case of carriage by sea or by more than one means of conveyance including carriage by sea, that the goods are or will be loaded on deck. Nevertheless, banks will accept a transport document which contains a provision that the goods may be carried on deck, provided that it does not specifically state that they are or will be loaded on deck,

and/or

ii. bears a clause on the face thereof such as "shipper's load and count" or "said by shipper to contain" or words of similar effect,

and/or

iii. indicates as the consignor of the goods a party other than the Beneficiary of the Credit.

Article 32

Clean Transport Documents

a A clean transport document is one which bears no clause or notation which expressly declares a defective condition of the goods and/or the packaging.

b Banks will not accept transport documents bearing such clauses or notations unless the Credit expressly stipulates the clauses or notations which may be accepted.

c Banks will regard a requirement in a Credit for a transport document to bear the clause "clean on board" as complied with if such transport document meets the requirements of this Article and of Articles 23, 24, 25, 26, 27, 28 or 30.

Article 33

Freight Payable/Prepaid Transport Documents

a Unless otherwise stipulated in the Credit, or inconsistent with any of the documents presented under the Credit, banks will accept transport documents stating that freight or transportation charges (hereafter referred to as "freight") have still to be paid.

b If a Credit stipulates that the transport document has to indicate that freight has been paid or prepaid, banks will accept a transport document on which words clearly indicating payment or prepayment of freight appear by stamp or otherwise, or on which payment or prepayment of freight is indicated by other means. If the Credit requires courier charges to be paid or prepaid banks will also accept a transport document issued by a courier or expedited delivery service evidencing that courier charges are for the account of a party other than the consignee.

c The words "freight prepayable" or "freight to be prepaid" or words of similar effect, if appearing on transport documents, will not be accepted as constituting evidence of the payment of freight.

d Banks will accept transport documents bearing reference by stamp or otherwise to costs additional to the freight, such as costs of, or disbursements incurred in connection with, loading, unloading or similar operations, unless the conditions of the Credit specifically prohibit such reference.

Article 34

Insurance Documents

a Insurance documents must appear on their face to be issued and signed by insurance companies or underwriters or their agents.

b If the insurance document indicates that it has been issued in more than one original, all the originals must be presented unless otherwise authorised in the Credit.

c Cover notes issued by brokers will not be accepted, unless specifically authorised in the Credit.

d Unless otherwise stipulated in the Credit, banks will accept an insurance certificate or a declaration under an open cover pre-signed by insurance companies or underwriters or their agents. If a Credit specifically calls for an insurance certificate or a declaration under an open cover, banks will accept, in lieu thereof, an insurance policy.

e Unless otherwise stipulated in the Credit, or unless it appears from the insurance document that the cover is effective at the latest from the date of loading on board or dispatch or taking in charge of the goods, banks will not accept an insurance document which bears a date of issuance later than the date of loading on board or dispatch or taking in charge as indicated in such transport document.

f   **i.**   Unless otherwise stipulated in the Credit, the insurance document must be expressed in the same currency as the Credit.

     ii.   Unless otherwise stipulated in the Credit, the minimum amount for which the insurance document must indicate the insurance cover to have been effected is the CIF (cost, insurance and freight (... "named port of destination")) or CIP (carriage and insurance paid to (..."named place of destination")) value of the goods, as the case may be, plus 10%, but only when the CIF or CIP value can be determined from the documents on their face. Otherwise, banks will accept as such minimum amount 110% of the amount for which payment, acceptance or negotiation is requested under the Credit, or 110% of the gross amount of the invoice, whichever is the greater.

Article 35

Type of Insurance Cover

a   Credits should stipulate the type of insurance required and, if any, the additional risks which are to be covered. Imprecise terms such as "usual risks" or "customary risks" shall not be used; if they are used, banks will accept insurance documents as presented, without responsibility for any risks not being covered.

b   Failing specific stipulations in the Credit, banks will accept insurance documents as presented, without responsibility for any risks not being covered.

c   Unless otherwise stipulated in the Credit, banks will accept an insurance document which indicates that the cover is subject to a franchise or an excess (deductible).

Article 36

All Risks Insurance Cover

Where a Credit stipulates "insurance against all risks", banks will accept an insurance document which contains any "all risks" notation or clause, whether or not bearing the heading "all risks", even if the insurance document indicates that certain risks are excluded, without responsibility for any risk(s) not being covered.

Article 37

Commercial Invoices

a   Unless otherwise stipulated in the Credit, commercial invoices;

   i.   must appear on their face to be issued by the Beneficiary named in the Credit (except as provided in Article 48),

   and

   ii.   must be made out in the name of the Applicant (except as provided in sub-Article 48 (h)),

   and

   iii.   need not be signed.

b   Unless otherwise stipulated in the Credit, banks may refuse commercial invoices issued for amounts in excess of the amount permitted by the Credit. Nevertheless, if a bank authorised to pay, incur a deferred payment undertaking, accept Draft(s), or negotiate under a Credit accepts such invoices, its decision will be binding upon all parties, provided that such bank has not paid, incurred a deferred payment undertaking, accepted Draft(s) or negotiated for an amount in excess of that permitted by the Credit.

c   The description of the goods in the commercial invoice must correspond with the description in the Credit. In all other documents, the goods may be described in general terms not inconsistent with the description of the goods in the Credit.

Article 38

Other Documents

If a Credit calls for an attestation or certification of weight in the case of transport other than by sea, banks will accept a weight stamp or declaration of weight which appears to have been superimposed on the transport document by the carrier or his agent unless the Credit specifically stipulates that the attestation or certification of weight must be by means of a separate document.

E. MISCELLANEOUS PROVISIONS

Article 39

Allowances in Credit Amount, Quantity and Unit Price

a The words "about", "approximately", "circa" or similar expressions used in connection with the amount of the Credit or the quantity or the unit price stated in the Credit are to be construed as allowing a difference not to exceed 10% more or 10% less than the amount or the quantity or the unit price to which they refer.

b Unless a Credit stipulates that the quantity of the goods specified must not be exceeded or reduced, a tolerance of 5% more or 5% less will be permissible, always provided that the amount of the drawings does not exceed the amount of the Credit. This tolerance does not apply when the Credit stipulates the quantity in terms of a stated number of packing units or individual items.

c Unless a Credit which prohibits partial shipments stipulates otherwise, or unless sub-Article (b) above is applicable, a tolerance of 5% less in the amount of the drawing will be permissible, provided that if the Credit stipulates the quantity of the goods, such quantity of goods is shipped in full, and if the Credit stipulates a unit price, such price is not reduced. This provision does not apply when expressions referred to in sub-Article (a) above are used in the Credit.

Article 40

Partial Shipments/Drawings

a Partial drawings and/or shipments are allowed, unless the Credit stipulates otherwise.

b Transport documents which appear on their face to indicate that shipment has been made on the same means of conveyance and for the same journey, provided they indicate the same destination, will not be regarded as covering partial shipments, even if the transport documents indicate different dates of shipment and/or different ports of loading, places of taking in charge, or despatch.

c Shipments made by post or by courier will not be regarded as partial shipments if the post receipts or certificates of posting or courier's receipts or dispatch notes appear to have been stamped, signed or otherwise authenticated in the place from which the Credit stipulates the goods are to be dispatched, and on the same date.

Article 41

Instalment Shipments/Drawings

If drawings and/or shipments by instalments within given periods are stipulated in the Credit and any instalment is not drawn and/or shipped within the period allowed for that instalment, the Credit ceases to be available for that and any subsequent instalments, unless otherwise stipulated in the Credit.

Article 42

Expiry Date and Place for Presentation of Documents

a All Credits must stipulate an expiry date and a place for presentation of documents for payment, acceptance, or with the exception of freely negotiable Credits, a place for presentation of documents for negotiation. An expiry date stipulated for payment, acceptance or negotiation will be construed to express an expiry date for presentation of documents.

b Except as provided in sub-Article 44(a), documents must be presented on or before such expiry date.

c If an Issuing Bank states that the Credit is to be available "for one month", "for six months", or the like, but does not specify the date from which the time is to run, the date of issuance of the Credit by the Issuing Bank will be deemed to be the first day from which such time is to run. Banks should discourage indication of the expiry date of the Credit in this manner.

Article 43

Limitation on the Expiry Date

a In addition to stipulating an expiry date for presentation of documents, every Credit which calls for a transport document(s) should also stipulate a specified period of time after the date of shipment during which presentation must be made in compliance with the terms and conditions of the Credit. If no such period of time is stipulated, banks will not accept documents presented to them later than 21 days after the date of shipment. In any event, documents must be presented not later than the expiry date of the Credit.

b In cases in which sub-Article 40(b) applies, the date of shipment will be considered to be the latest shipment date on any of the transport documents presented.

Article 44

Extension of Expiry Date

a If the expiry date of the Credit and/or the last day of the period of time for presentation of documents stipulated by the Credit or applicable by virtue of Article 43 falls on a day on which the bank to which presentation has to be made is closed for reasons other than those referred to in Article 17, the stipulated expiry date and/ or the last day of the period of time after the date of shipment for presentation of documents, as the case may be, shall be extended to the first following day on which such bank is open.

b The latest date for shipment shall not be extended by reason of the extension of the expiry date and/or the period of time after the date of shipment for presentation of documents in accordance with sub-Article (a) above. If no such latest date for shipment is stipulated in the Credit or amendments thereto, banks will not accept transport documents indicating a date of shipment later than the expiry date stipulated in the Credit or amendments thereto.

c The bank to which presentation is made on such first following business day must provide a statement that the documents were presented within the time limits extended in accordance with sub-Article 44(a) of the Uniform Customs and Practice for Documentary Credits, 1993 Revision, ICC Publication No. 500.

Article 45

Hours of Presentation

Banks are under no obligation to accept presentation of documents outside their banking hours.

Article 46

General Expressions as to Dates for Shipment

a Unless otherwise stipulated in the Credit, the expression "shipment" used in stipulating an earliest and/or a latest date for shipment will be understood to include expressions such as, "loading on board", "dispatch", "accepted for carriage", "date of post receipt", "date of pick-up", and the like, and in the case of a Credit calling for a multimodal transport document the expression "taking in charge".

b Expressions such as "prompt", "immediately", "as soon as possible", and the like should not be used. If they are used banks will disregard them.

c If the expression "on or about" or similar expressions are used, banks will interpret them as a stipulation that shipment is to be made during the period from five days before to five days after the specified date, both end days included.

Article 47

Date Terminology for Periods of Shipment

a The words "to", "until", "till", "from" and words of similar import applying to any date or period in the Credit referring to shipment will be understood to include the date mentioned.

b The word "after" will be understood to exclude the date mentioned.

c The terms "first half", "second half" of a month shall be construed respectively as the 1st to the 15th, and the 16th to the last day of such month, all dates inclusive.

d The terms "beginning", "middle", or "end" of a month shall be construed respectively as the 1st to the 10th, the 11th to the 20th, and the 21st to the last day of such month, all dates inclusive.

F. TRANSFERABLE CREDIT

Article 48

Transferable Credit

a A transferable Credit is a Credit under which the Beneficiary (First Beneficiary) may request the bank authorised to pay, incur a deferred payment undertaking, accept or negotiate (the "Transferring Bank"), or in the case of a freely negotiable Credit, the bank specifically authorised in the Credit as a Transferring Bank, to make the Credit available in whole or in part to one or more other Beneficiary(ies) (Second Beneficiary(ies)).

b A Credit can be transferred only if it is expressly designated as "transferable" by the Issuing Bank. Terms such as "divisible", "fractionable", "assignable", and "transmissible" do not render the Credit transferable. If such terms are used they shall be disregarded.

c The Transferring Bank shall be under no obligation to effect such transfer except to the extent and in the manner expressly consented to by such bank.

d At the time of making a request for transfer and prior to transfer of the Credit, the First Beneficiary must irrevocably instruct the Transferring Bank whether or not he retains the right to refuse to allow the Transferring Bank to advise amendments to the Second Beneficiary(ies). If the Transferring Bank consents to the transfer under these conditions, it must, at the time of transfer, advise the Second Beneficiary(ies) of the First Beneficiary's instructions regarding amendments.

e If a Credit is transferred to more than one Second Beneficiary(ies), refusal of an amendment by one or more Second Beneficiary(ies) does not invalidate the acceptance(s) by the other Second Beneficiary(ies) with respect to whom the Credit will be amended accordingly. With respect to the Second Beneficiary(ies) who rejected the amendment, the Credit will remain unamended.

f Transferring Bank charges in respect of transfers including commissions, fees, costs or expenses are payable by the First Beneficiary, unless otherwise agreed. If the Transferring Bank agrees to transfer the Credit it shall be under no obligation to effect the transfer until such charges are paid.

g Unless otherwise stated in the Credit, a transferable Credit can be transferred once only. Consequently, the Credit cannot be transferred at the request of the Second Beneficiary to any subsequent Third Beneficiary. For the purpose of this Article, a retransfer to the First Beneficiary does not constitute a prohibited transfer.

Fractions of a transferable Credit (not exceeding in the aggregate the amount of the Credit) can be transferred separately, provided partial shipments/drawings are not prohibited, and the aggregate of such transfers will be considered as constituting only one transfer of the Credit.

h The Credit can be transferred only on the terms and conditions specified in the original Credit, with the exception of:

- the amount of the Credit,
- any unit price stated therein,
- the expiry date,
- the last date for presentation of documents in accordance with Article 43,
- the period for shipment,

any or all of which may be reduced or curtailed.

The percentage for which insurance cover must be effected may be increased in such a way as to provide the amount of cover stipulated in the original Credit, or these Articles.

In addition, the name of the First Beneficiary can be substituted for that of the Applicant, but if the name of the Applicant is specifically required by the original Credit to appear in any document(s) other than the invoice, such requirement must be fulfilled.

i The First Beneficiary has the right to substitute his own invoice(s) (and Draft(s)) for those of the Second Beneficiary(ies), for amounts not in excess of the original amount stipulated in the Credit and for the original unit prices if stipulated in the Credit, and upon such substitution of invoice(s) (and Draft(s)) the First Beneficiary can draw under the Credit for the difference, if any, between his invoice(s) and the Second Beneficiary's(ies') invoice(s).

When a Credit has been transferred and the First Beneficiary is to supply his own invoice(s) (and Draft(s)) in exchange for the Second Bene-ficiary's(ies') invoice(s) (and Draft(s)) but fails to do so on first demand, the Transferring Bank has the right to deliver to the Issuing Bank the documents received under the transferred Credit, including the Second Beneficiary's(ies') invoice(s) (and Draft(s)) without further responsibility to the First Beneficiary.

j The First Beneficiary may request that payment or negotiation be effected to the Second Beneficiary(ies) at the place to which the Credit has been transferred up to and including the expiry date of the Credit, unless the original Credit expressly states that it may not be made available for payment or negotiation at a place other than that stipulated in the Credit. This is without prejudice to the First Beneficiary's right to substitute subsequently his own invoice(s) (and Draft(s)) for those of the Second Beneficiary(ies) and to claim any difference due to him.

G. ASSIGNMENT OF PROCEEDS

Article 49

Assignment of Proceeds

The fact that a Credit is not stated to be transferable shall not affect the Beneficiary's right to assign any proceeds to which he may be, or may become, entitled under such Credit, in accordance with the provisions of the applicable law. This Article relates only to the assignment of proceeds and not to the assignment of the right to perform under the Credit itself.

Supplement to UCP 500 for Electronic Presentation

in force as of 1 April 2002

Version 1.0

PREFACE

The completion of the UCP Supplement for Electronic Presentation (eUCP) brings the documentary credit into the electronic age. It recognizes that while electronic documents are still relatively new, they represent the way of the future. And it positions the ICC – which has established rules on documentary credits for more than 60 years – to maintain its pre-eminent role in setting standards in the field.

A supplement to, and not a replacement of the UCP, the eUCP has been written to allow UCP 500 and eUCP to work together. The new supplement provides helpful definitions of terms that have different meanings in the electronic and paper worlds. Terms such as "appears on its face", "place for presentation" and "sign" are redefined in the eUCP to take account of the electronic environment.

The eUCP also address other key issues of electronic presentation, among them:

- The format in which electronic records are to be presented;
- The consequences if a bank is open but its system is unable to receive an electronic record;
- How notice of refusal of an electronic record is to be handled;
- How original documents are to be defined in the electronic world; and
- What happens when an electronic record is corrupted by a virus or other defect.

The publication of the eUCP is a watershed event in the history of the documentary credit. Clearly, future UCP revisions will have to take into account the growing use of electronic documents and the trend towards electronic trade. This will mean that professionals working in the field will have to make adjustments and that rule makers will have to give them the legal framework within which they can do their jobs.

While the paper-based credit is likely to be with us for some time to come, no one working with documentary credits can afford to ignore the new realities of our age – internet sites that promise to handle a trade transaction from start to finish; imaging techniques that allow documents to be "signed" and transmitted directly to customers; and new software that simplifies the work of applicants, beneficiaries and document checkers alike.

But whether credits are paper-based or electronic, the new world of trade finance will still require a framework of rules that all the parties can have confidence in. ICC has provided that framework since the 1930s. The development of the eUCP guarantees that it will continue to do so in the years ahead.

I want to thank all members of the working group (listed on the following page) who made this text possible and to offer special thanks to Dan Taylor (US) and Rene Müller (Switzerland) for the superb job they did in co-chairing this fine effort.

Dieter Kiefer
Chairman
ICC Banking Commission
December 2001

WORKING GROUP ON THE UCP SUPPLEMENT FOR ELECTRONIC PRESENTATION (eUCP)

Co-Chairmen

Dan Taylor (US), President, International Financial Services Association and René Müller (Switzerland), Director, Trade Finance, Credit Suisse

Members

Prof. James E. Byrne (US), Director, Institute of International Banking Law & Practice and George Mason University School of Law

William. I. Cameron (Canada), General Manager, Trade Finance-Identrus Project, Canadian Imperial Bank of Commerce

Kim Chalmer (Denmark), General Manager, E-Commerce, Maersk (A.P. Møller)

Gabriel Chami (Lebanon), Legal & Technical Adviser, Banque Audi SAL

Neil J. Chantry (UK), Manager Policy and Procedures, Group Trade Services, HSBC Holdings plc

Gary Collyer (UK), Vice-President, European Trade Business Management, Citibank International Plc

Dr Carlo Di Ninni, (Italy), Manager, Documentary Credit Department, Associazione Bancaria Italiana

Johannes M. Fritzen (Germany), President, Volkswagen Transport GMBH & Co. OHG

Winfried Holzwarth (Germany), Counsel, Deutsche Bank AG – Frankfurt

Ms Nicole Keller (Germany), Product Manager, International Business, Dresdner Bank AG – Frankfurt

Ms Laurence Kooy (France), International Legal Affairs, Head of Global Trade Services, BNP Paribas

Fredrik Lundberg (Sweden), Senior Trade Finance Adviser, Nordea Bank Sverige AB – Stockholm

Avv. Salvatore Maccarone (Italy), Professor of Law, Maccarone & Associati Studio Legale

Vincent M. Maulella (US), International Banking Advisor, US Council for International Business

David Meynell (UK), Vice President, Trade Services, Deutsche Bank

Paul Miserez (Belgium), Head of Trade Finance Standards, SWIFT

Vincent O'Brien (Ireland), Documentary Credit Specialist, Obrico Ltd

Bhaskar Yashwant Olkar (India), Chief Executive, Foreign Exchange Dealers' Association of India

Arthur O. Thomas (US), former Global Manager of Trade & Regulatory Affairs, APL Limited

INTRODUCTION

At its meeting on 24 May 2000 in Paris, the Task Force on the Future of the Commission on Banking Technique and Practice ("Banking Commission") set as one of its goals a greater focus on electronic trade. Further discussion identified a need to develop a bridge between the current UCP 500 and the processing of the electronic equivalent of paper-based credits. While the UCP have been extremely successful over their 60-year history in providing self-regulation for the letter of credit industry, the need was apparent to update the rules to accommodate technological changes.

With the current evolution from paper to electronic credits, it was determined that the market was looking to the ICC to provide guidance in this transition. In response, the Banking Commission established a Working Group consisting of experts in the UCP, electronic trade, legal issues and related industries, such as transport, to prepare the appropriate rules as a "supplement" to the UCP. The Commission approved this recommendation, and the result of 18 months of intense effort by the Working Group is the new Supplement to the Uniform Customs and Practice for Documentary Credits for Electronic Presentation or "eUCP".

The eUCP is *not* a revision of the UCP. The UCP will continue to provide the industry with rules for paper letters of credit for many years. The eUCP is a *supplement* to the UCP that, when used in conjunction with the UCP, will provide the necessary rules for the presentation of the electronic equivalents of paper documents under letters of credit.

The eUCP provide definitions to allow current UCP terminology to accommodate electronic presentation and the necessary rules to allow the UCP and the eUCP to work together. The eUCP have been written to allow for presentation completely electronically or for a mixture of paper documents and electronic presentation. Although the practice is evolving, providing exclusively for electronic presentation is not entirely realistic at this time, nor will it promote the transition to total electronic presentation.

The eUCP does *not* address any issues relating to the *issuance or advice* of credits electronically, since current market practice and the UCP have long allowed for this to be done. In this respect, it is important for users of the eUCP to understand that many Articles of the UCP are not impacted by the electronic presentation of the equivalent of paper documents and do not require any changes to accommodate it. When read together, the UCP and the eUCP are broad enough to allow for developing practice in this field.

The eUCP is specific to UCP 500 and, if necessary, may have to be revised as technologies develop, perhaps prior to the next revision of the UCP. For that reason, the eUCP are issued in version numbers that will allow for a revision and subsequent version if the need arises. The current version is Version 1.0.

The eUCP have been drafted to be independent of specific technologies and developing electronic commerce systems; in other words, they do not address or define the specific technologies or systems necessary to facilitate electronic presentation. These technologies are evolving and the eUCP leave the parties free to agree on the technology or systems to be used. Nor do the eUCP specify the format – for example, e-mail or one of the various document processing programmes – to be used in the transmission of electronic messages. This too is for the parties to decide.

All of the Articles of the eUCP are consistent with the UCP except as they relate specifically to electronic presentations. Where necessary, changes have been made in the eUCP to address the differences between presentations in paper and electronic form.

In order to avoid confusion between the Articles of the UCP and the eUCP, the Articles of the eUCP are numbered with an "e" preceding each Article number.

For credits allowing for the presentation of electronic documents (or a mixture of paper and electronic), it will be necessary to specifically incorporate the eUCP if the parties wish them to apply. It is *not* necessary to incorporate both the UCP and eUCP, since the supplement incorporates the UCP in any credit subject to it.

I would like to thank my co-Chair of the eUCP Working Group, René Müller, for his invaluable assistance in this process. I would also like to thank all of the members of the Working Group for their belief in this project and their dedication to it. The Working Group also expresses its appreciation to all of the ICC national committees and individuals who provided comments during this process. Without their input, it would not have been possible to produce this supplement.

Dan Taylor, Co-Chair, eUCP Working Group
Vice Chair of the ICC Banking Commission and
President, International Financial Services Association

SUPPLEMENT TO UCP 500
FOR ELECTRONIC PRESENTATION – VERSION 1.0

Article e1
Scope of the eUCP

a   The Supplement to the Uniform Customs and Practice for Documentary Credits for Electronic Presentation ("eUCP") supplements the Uniform Customs and Practice for Documentary Credits (1993 Revision ICC Publication No. 500,) ("UCP") in order to accommodate presentation of electronic records alone or in combination with paper documents.

b   The eUCP shall apply as a supplement to the UCP where the Credit indicates that it is subject to eUCP.

c   This version is Version 1.0. A Credit must indicate the applicable version of the eUCP. If it does not do so, it is subject to the version in effect on the date the Credit is issued or, if made subject to eUCP by an amendment accepted by the Beneficiary, on the date of that amendment.

Article e2
Relationship of the eUCP to the UCP

a   A Credit subject to the eUCP ("eUCP Credit") is also subject to the UCP without express incorporation of the UCP.

b   Where the eUCP applies, its provisions shall prevail to the extent that they would produce a result different from the application of the UCP.

c   If an eUCP Credit allows the Beneficiary to choose between presentation of paper documents or electronic records and it chooses to present only paper documents, the UCP alone shall apply to that presentation. If only paper documents are permitted under an eUCP Credit, the UCP alone shall apply.

Article e3

Definitions

a Where the following terms are used in the UCP, for the purposes of applying the UCP to an electronic record presented under an eUCP Credit, the term:

   i. "**appears on its face**" and the like shall apply to examination of the data content of an electronic record.

   ii. "**document**" shall include an electronic record.

   iii. "**place for presentation**" of electronic records means an electronic address.

   iv. "**sign**" and the like shall include an electronic signature.

   v. "**superimposed**", "**notation**" or "**stamped**" means data content whose supplementary character is apparent in an electronic record.

b The following terms used in the eUCP shall have the following meanings:

   i. "**electronic record**" means

- data created, generated, sent, communicated, received, or stored by electronic means

- that is capable of being authenticated as to the apparent identity of a sender and the apparent source of the data contained in it, and as to whether it has remained complete and unaltered, and

- is capable of being examined for compliance with the terms and conditions of the eUCP Credit.

   ii. "**electronic signature**" means a data process attached to or logically associated with an electronic record and executed or adopted by a person in order to identify that person and to indicate that person's authentication of the electronic record.

   iii. "**format**" means the data organisation in which the electronic record is expressed or to which it refers.

   iv. "**paper document**" means a document in a traditional paper form.

   v. "**received**" means the time when an electronic record enters the information system of the applicable recipient in a form capable of being accepted by that system. Any acknowledgement of receipt does not imply acceptance or refusal of the electronic record under an eUCP Credit.

Article e4

Format

An eUCP Credit must specify the formats in which electronic records are to be presented. If the format of the electronic record is not so specified, it may be presented in any format.

Article e5

Presentation

a An eUCP Credit allowing presentation of:

    i. electronic records must state a place for presentation of the electronic records.

    ii. both electronic records and paper documents must also state a place for presentation of the paper documents.

b Electronic records may be presented separately and need not be presented at the same time.

c If an eUCP Credit allows for presentation of one or more electronic records, the Beneficiary is responsible for providing a notice to the Bank to which presentation is made signifying when the presentation is complete. The notice of completeness may be given as an electronic record or paper document and must identify the eUCP Credit to which it relates. Presentation is deemed not to have been made if the Beneficiary's notice is not received.

d **i.** Each presentation of an electronic record and the presentation of paper documents under an eUCP Credit must identify the eUCP Credit under which it is presented.

    ii. A presentation not so identified may be treated as not received.

e   If the Bank to which presentation is to be made is open but its system is unable to receive a transmitted electronic record on the stipulated expiry date and/or the last day of the period of time after the date of shipment for presentation, as the case may be, the Bank will be deemed to be closed and the date for presentation and/or the expiry date shall be extended to the first following banking day on which such Bank is able to receive an electronic record. If the only electronic record remaining to be presented is the notice of completeness, it may be given by telecommunications or by paper document and will be deemed timely, provided that it is sent before the bank is able to receive an electronic record.

f   An electronic record that cannot be authenticated is deemed not to have been presented.

Article e6
Examination

a   If an electronic record contains a hyperlink to an external system or a presentation indicates that the electronic record may be examined by reference to an external system, the electronic record at the hyperlink or the referenced system shall be deemed to be the electronic record to be examined. The failure of the indicated system to provide access to the required electronic record at the time of examination shall constitute a discrepancy.

b   The forwarding of electronic records by a Nominated Bank pursuant to its nomination signifies that it has checked the apparent authenticity of the electronic records.

c   The inability of the Issuing Bank, or Confirming Bank, if any, to examine an electronic record in a format required by the eUCP Credit or, if no format is required, to examine it in the format presented is not a basis for refusal.

Article e7

Notice of Refusal

a **i.** The time period for the examination of documents commences on the banking day following the banking day on which the Beneficiary's notice of completeness is received.

   ii. If the time for presentation of documents or the notice of completeness is extended, the time for the examination of documents commences on the first following banking day on which the bank to which presentation is to be made is able to receive the notice of completeness.

b If an Issuing Bank, the Confirming Bank, if any, or a Nominated Bank acting on their behalf, provides a notice of refusal of a presentation which includes electronic records and does not receive instructions from the party to which notice of refusal is given within 30 calendar days from the date the notice of refusal is given for the disposition of the electronic records, the Bank shall return any paper documents not previously returned to the presenter but may dispose of the electronic records in any manner deemed appropriate without any responsibility.

Article e8

Originals and Copies

Any requirement of the UCP or an eUCP Credit for presentation of one or more originals or copies of an electronic record is satisfied by the presentation of one electronic record.

Article e9

Date of Issuance

Unless an electronic record contains a specific date of issuance, the date on which it appears to have been sent by the issuer is deemed to be the date of issuance. The date of receipt will be deemed to be the date it was sent if no other date is apparent.

Article e10
Transport

If an electronic record evidencing transport does not indicate a date of shipment or dispatch, the date of issuance of the electronic record will be deemed to be the date of shipment or dispatch. However, if the electronic record bears a notation that evidences the date of shipment or dispatch, the date of the notation will be deemed to be the date of shipment or dispatch. A notation showing additional data content need not be separately signed or otherwise authenticated.

Article e11
Corruption of an Electronic Record after Presentation

a If an electronic record that has been received by the Issuing Bank, Confirming Bank, or another Nominated Bank appears to have been corrupted, the Bank may inform the presenter and may request that the electronic record be re-presented.

b If the Bank requests that an electronic record be re-presented:

i. the time for examination is suspended and resumes when the presenter re-presents the electronic record; and

ii. if the Nominated Bank is not the Confirming Bank, it must provide the Issuing Bank and any Confirming Bank with notice of the request for re-presentation and inform it of the suspension; but

iii. if the same electronic record is not re-presented within thirty (30) calendar days, the Bank may treat the electronic record as not presented, and

iv. any deadlines are not extended.

Article e12

Additional Disclaimer of Liability for Presentation of Electronic Records under eUCP

By checking the apparent authenticity of an electronic record, Banks assume no liability for the identity of the sender, source of the information, or its complete and unaltered character other than that which is apparent in the electronic record received by the use of a commercially acceptable data process for the receipt, authentication, and identification of electronic records.

ICC Banking Commission
Decisions & Policy Statements

THE DETERMINATION OF AN "ORIGINAL" DOCUMENT IN THE CONTEXT OF UCP 500 SUB-ARTICLE 20(b)

Commission on Banking Technique and Practice, 12 July 1999

Original documents

This Decision emphasizes the need to correctly interpret and apply sub-Article 20(b) of UCP 500. Consequently, ICC national committees and associated organizations are strongly urged to distribute this Decision as widely as possible to help ensure the correct interpretation in the evaluation of documents issued under letters of credit. This Decision does not amend sub-Article 20(b) of UCP 500 in any way, but merely indicates the correct interpretation thereof which has been adopted unanimously by the ICC Commission on Banking Technique and Practice on 12 July 1999.

1. Background

Over a period of several years there have been a number of queries raised with the ICC Banking Commission as to the determination, by banks, of what is an "original" document under a letter of credit and the necessity, if any, for such a document to be so marked.

For ease of reference the text of sub-Article 20(b) reads:

> "Unless otherwise stipulated in the Credit, banks will also accept as an original document(s), a document(s) produced or appearing to have been produced
> * by reprographic, automated or computerized systems
> * as carbon copies;
>
> provided that it is marked as original and, where necessary, appears to be signed.
>
> A document may be signed by handwriting, by facsimile signature, by perforated signature, by stamp, by symbol, or by any other mechanical or electronic method of authentication."

2. Determination of originality

In documentary credit operations, the document checker is faced with a number of issues pertaining to originality including:

Apparent originality
Banks undertake to determine whether a document appears on its face to be an original document, as distinguished from a copy. Except as expressly required by a letter of credit including an incorporated term – such as UCP 500 sub-Articles 23(a)(iv) or 34(b) – banks do not undertake to determine whether an apparent original is the sole original. Banks rely on the apparent intent of the issuer of the document that it be treated as an original rather than a copy.

In this regard, a person sending a telefax or making a photocopy on plain paper or pressing through carbon paper presumably intends to produce a copy. On the other hand, a person printing a document on plain paper from a text that that person created and electronically stored presumably intends to produce an original. Accordingly, documents bearing facsimile signatures or printed in their entirety (even including the issuer's letterhead and/or signature) from electronically stored text are presumably intended by the document issuer to be original and in practice are accepted by banks as original.

Documents that appear to be original but are not
Banks do not undertake to determine whether a document is original in fact. Under UCP 500 Article 15, banks are not responsible for the genuineness or falsification of any document. If a document appears to be original or to have been marked as original but is in fact not original, then its presentation may give rise to exceptional defences, rights, or obligations under the law applicable to forged or fraudulent presentations and is beyond the scope of UCP 500.

UCP 500 requirements
The UCP neither requires nor permits an examination beyond the face of a document to determine how the document was in fact produced, unless the document was produced by the bank, e.g. on a telefax, telex, e-mail, or other system that prints out messages received by the bank. The "produced or appearing to have been produced" language in sub-Article 20(b) does not override UCP 500 sub-Articles 13(a), 13(c), or 14(b), or other practice and law that prohibit issuers and confirmers from determining compliance on the basis of extrinsic facts.

As indicated by inclusion of the word "also" (" ... banks will also accept as original(s) ..."), sub-Article 20(b) is neither comprehensive nor exclusive in its provisions that distinguish originals from copies. For example, a document printed on plain paper from electronically stored text is acceptable, without regard to 20(b), if it appears to be an original.

Sub-Article 20(b) does not apply to documents that appear to be only partially produced by reprographic, automated, or computerized systems or as carbon copies. In this regard, a photocopy ceases to be "reprographically produced" within the meaning of sub-Article 20(b) when it is also manually stamped, dated, completed, or signed by the issuer of the document.

The "marked as original" proviso in sub-Article 20(b) is satisfied by any marking on a document or any recital in the text of a document that indicates that the issuer of the document intends it to be treated as an original rather than a copy. Accordingly, a document that appears to have been printed on plain paper from electronically stored text is "marked as original" under sub-Article 20(b) if it also states that it is original or includes letterhead or is hand marked.

Sub-Article 13(a) of UCP 500 refers to compliance of the presented documents being determined by international standard banking practice as defined in the articles of UCP. International standard banking practice in relation to determination of "original" documents could be described as follows:

3. Correct interpretation of sub-Article 20(b)

General approach
Banks examine documents presented under a letter of credit to determine, among other things, whether on their face they appear to be original. Banks treat as original any document bearing an apparently original signature, mark, stamp, or label of the issuer of the document, unless the document itself indicates that it is not original. Accordingly, unless a document indicates otherwise, it is treated as original if it:

(A) appears to be written, typed, perforated, or stamped by the document issuer's hand; or

(B) appears to be on the document issuer's original stationery; or

(C) states that it is original, unless the statement appears not to apply to the document presented (e.g. because it appears to be a photocopy of another document and the statement of originality appears to apply to that other document).

Hand signed documents

Consistent with sub-paragraph (A) above, banks treat as original any document that appears to be hand signed by the issuer of the document. For example, a hand signed draft or commercial invoice is treated as an original document, whether or not some or all other constituents of the document are preprinted, carbon copied, or produced by reprographic, automated, or computerized systems.

Facsimile signed documents

Banks treat a facsimile signature as the equivalent of a hand signature. Accordingly, a document that appears to bear the document issuer's facsimile signature is also treated as an original document.

Photocopies

Banks treat as non-original any document that appears to be a photocopy of another document. If, however, a photocopy appears to have been completed by the document issuer's hand marking the photocopy, then, consistent with sub-paragraph (A) above, the resulting document is treated as an original document unless it indicates otherwise. If a document appears to have been produced by photocopying text onto original stationery rather than onto blank paper, then, consistent with sub-paragraph (B) above, it is treated as an original document unless it indicates otherwise.

Telefaxed presentation of documents

Banks treat as non-original any document that is produced at the bank's telefax machine. A letter of credit that permits presentation by telefax waives any requirement for presentation of an original of any document presented by telefax.

Statements indicating originality

Consistent with either or both of sub-paragraphs (A) and (C) above, a document on which the word "original" has been stamped is treated as an original document. A statement in a document that it is a "duplicate original" or the "third of three" also indicates that it is original. Originality is also indicated by a statement in a document that it is void if another document of the same tenor and date is used.

Statements indicating non-originality

A statement in a document that it is a true copy of another document or that another document is the sole original indicates that it is not original. A statement in a document that it is the "customer's copy" or "shipper's copy" neither disclaims nor affirms its originality.

4. What is not an "Original"?

A document indicates that it is not an original if it

- appears to be produced on a telefax machine;

- appears to be a photocopy of another document which has not otherwise been completed by hand marking the photocopy or by photocopying it on what appears to be original stationery; or

- states in the document that it is a true copy of another document or that another document is the sole original.

5. Conclusion

Based upon the comments received from ICC national committees, members of the ICC Banking Commission and other interested parties, the statements in clauses 3 and 4 above reflect international standard banking practice in the correct interpretation of UCP 500 sub-Article 20(b).

ICC ENDORSEMENT OF THE UNCITRAL CONVENTION ON INDEPENDENT GUARANTEES AND STAND-BY LETTERS OF CREDIT

Commission on Banking Technique and Practice, 21 June 1999

On the unanimous consent of its Commission on Banking Technique and Practice, the International Chamber of Commerce endorses the United Nations Convention on Independent Guarantees and Stand-by Letters of Credit.

Since its earliest years, ICC has provided important international leadership in the field of international banking operations, particularly as a forum for developing rules of practice. Since 1933, the Uniform Customs and Practice for Documentary Credits (UCP), in its various revisions, has become a universally recognized standard, stating and establishing custom and practice for letters of credit.

In this process, the United Nations Commission on International Trade Law (UNCITRAL), by its endorsement of the subsequent UCP versions, provided an important bridge to those countries who were at the time unable to participate directly in the work of ICC. Other ICC rules, such as Incoterms, have also been endorsed by UNCITRAL, which has contributed to their international acceptance.

ICC rules cannot be fully effective in all countries without their being recognized under local law. In this respect, the recent work of UNCITRAL on the United Nations Convention on Independent Guarantees and Stand-by Letters of Credit provides an important impetus to attain this objective. The Convention sets forth the basic principles of law for independent undertakings in a manner which fully assures their independent nature, which guarantees widest possible party autonomy and which establishes a uniform international legal standard for limits to the exception for fraudulent or abusive drawings.

ICC appreciates that the Convention was drafted in full recognition of the role of the various ICC rules in this field, that the UNCITRAL Working Group was directly and indirectly influenced by, and in turn influenced, the revision of the UCP, ICC's Uniform Rules for Demand Guarantees (URDG) and its recently adopted rules on International Standby Practices (ISP 98). ICC also notes that the UN Convention expressly defers to international banking practice as represented by ICC rules.

THE IMPACT OF THE EUROPEAN SINGLE CURRENCY (euro) ON MONETARY OBLIGATIONS RELATED TO TRANSACTIONS INVOLVING ICC RULES

Commission on Banking Technique and Practice, 6 April 1998

The International Chamber of Commerce (ICC) is the world business organization, based in Paris. The ICC Commissions on Banking Technique & Practice, International Commercial Practice, and Insurance, develop and maintain uniform rules for international trade, including the Uniform Rules for Contract Guarantees (URCG 325), Uniform Rules for Demand Guarantees (URDG 458), Uniform Customs and Practice for Documentary Credits (UCP 500), Uniform Rules for Collections (URC 522), Uniform Rules for Contract Bonds (URCB 524), and Uniform Rules for Bank-to-Bank Reimbursements (URR 525) (hereinafter referred to collectively as "ICC Rules").

The Introduction of the European single currency (euro), shall not have the effect of altering, discharging or excusing performance under any instrument subject to ICC Rules. This Decision emphasizes the need to correctly interpret and apply ICC Rules. Consequently, ICC national committees and associated organizations are strongly urged to distribute this Decision as widely as possible to help ensure the future smooth running of the instruments issued under ICC Rules. This Decision does not amend any articles of ICC Rules in any way, but merely indicates the correct interpretation thereof which has been adopted unanimously by the ICC Commission on Banking Technique and Practice, on 6 April 1998.

1. General

1.1 As of 1 January 1999, the euro will be substituted for the national currency unit of those European Union member states participating in European Economic and Monetary Union (hereinafter, "EMU-Participating States") which are to be designated in May 1998. During the transitional period running from 1 January 1999 to 31 December 2001, the euro (1 euro = 100 cents) will also be divided into the national currency unit of the EMU-Participating States according to conversion rates which are to be irrevocably fixed by the Council of the European Union as of 1 January 1999 ("conversion rates"). The term "national currency unit" as used below refers to the currency of any EMU-Participating State before 1 January 1999.

During the transitional period persons are free to use either the euro or the national currency unit, but will not (unless otherwise agreed) be obliged to receive or make payment in euro. Any amount denominated either in euro or in a national currency unit of a given EMU-Participating State and payable within that state by crediting an account of the creditor, may be paid by the debtor either in euro or in that national currency unit, with any necessary conversion being effected at the conversion rate.

As of 1 January 1999 the ECU will be replaced by the euro at the rate of one euro to one ECU.

1.2 As from 1 January 2002 the national currency unit will cease to exist and the euro will be the only legal currency in the EMU-Participating States; all payments must be in euro.

1.3 Continuity of contract will not be affected by the introduction of the euro.

1.4 The above principles affecting national currency unit are legally binding in all EMU-Participating States, and apply equally to payment to be made in a national currency unit by persons located outside the European Union, due to the generally accepted legal principle that the definition of what constitutes legal tender is governed by the law of the country whose currency is involved (sometimes referred to as the *lex monetae* principle).

2. Consequences of the introduction of the euro on practice under various ICC rules

2.1 UCP 500 for Documentary Credits (including standby letters of credit). *Below are the different possible cases and the relevant rules of interpretation:*

2.1.1 Documentary credits issued and payable before 1 January 1999 in a national currency unit.

Payment must be made and documents denominated in the currency of the credit.

2.1.2 Documentary credits issued before 1 January 1999 and payable between 1 January 1999 and 1 January 2002 in a national currency unit .

Payment must be made in the currency of the credit, but documents issued between 1 January 1999 and 1 January 2002 may be presented either in the currency of the credit or in the euro equivalent or in the equivalent cross-value in the national currency unit of the beneficiary's place of business; however, where payment is to be made in the currency of an EMU-Participating State and by crediting an account located in such member state, payment may at the debtor's (e.g. issuing bank's) option be effected in the euro equivalent.

2.1.3 Documentary credits issued in a national currency unit before 1 January 1999 and payable on or after 1 January 2002.

Payment must be made in euro, but documents issued between 1 January 1999 and 1 January 2002 may be presented either in the currency of the credit or in the euro equivalent or in the equivalent cross-value in the national currency unit of the beneficiary's place of business; documents issued on or after 1 January 2002 must be denominated in euro.

2.1.4 Documentary credits issued and payable on or after 1 January 1999 and before 1 January 2002 in a national currency unit or in euro.

Payment must be made in the currency of the credit, but documents issued between 1 January 1999 and 1 January 2002 may be presented in the currency of the credit or in the euro equivalent or in the equivalent cross-value in the national currency unit at the beneficiary's place of business; however, where the currency of the credit is a national currency unit and payment is to be made in the currency of a particular EMU-Participating State by crediting an account located in such member state, payment may at the debtor's (e.g. issuing bank's) option be effected in euro.

2.1.5 Documentary credits issued on or after 1 January 1999 but before 1 January 2002 in a national currency unit or in euro and payable on or after 1 January 2002.

Payment must be made in euro, but documents may be presented either in the currency of the credit or, as the case may be, in euro or in the national currency unit of the beneficiary's place of business, provided always that documents issued on or after 1 January 2002 must be denominated in euro.

2.1.6 For purposes of examples 2.1.2, 2.1.3, 2.1.4 and 2.1.5 above, documents (including insurance documents mentioned in UCP Art. 34 f) are not considered as being inconsistent with one another, if, within a single presentation of documents, any documents are denominated in the currency of the credit and/or in euro and/or in the national currency unit of the beneficiary's place of business.

2.1.7 Documentary credits issued and payable on or after 1 January 2002.

Credits cannot be issued in a national currency unit and must be issued in euro and payment must be made and documents (issued on or after 1 January 2002) denominated in euro.

2.1.8 The guidelines set forth in this Decision apply equally to transferable credits. With regard to transferable credits issued in a national currency unit and to be transferred during the transitional period, the transferring bank may convert the currency and amount of the credit into the euro equivalent.

2.2 URCG 325 / URDG 458 / URCB 524 — Guarantees and bonds

The principles set forth above also apply to guarantees and bonds.

2.3 URC 522 Collections

Collections must be made in the currency stipulated in the collection instructions. However, if a collection instruction stipulates a national currency unit of an EMU-Participating State, as of 1 January 1999 payment may be made in the euro equivalent and as of 1 January 2002, payment must be made and accepted in the euro equivalent.

2.4 URR 525 Bank-to-Bank Reimbursements

Reimbursement claims must be made and honoured in the currency of the reimbursement authorization or reimbursement undertaking. However, if such currency is the national currency unit of an EMU-Participating State, from 1 January 1999 they may be made and honoured in the euro equivalent, and as from 1 January 2002 they must be made and honoured in the euro equivalent.

Selected Opinions of the ICC Banking Commission on UCP 500

SUB-ARTICLE 9(d)(iii)   R 315

Whether an issuing bank and/or advising bank can give a deadline for the notification of an amendment

Query

We would like to have an interpretation of sub-Article 9(d) of UCP 500. Bank I issued an irrevocable L/C to the beneficiary through the advising/negotiating bank, Bank A, and subsequently issued an amendment to the original terms.

The beneficiary failed to give notification of acceptance or rejection of the amendment. The documents received by Bank A were in full compliance with the terms and conditions of the original L/C.

The questions are:

1) In this situation, should we deem that the beneficiary has rejected the amendment?

2) Could the issuing bank and/or advising bank give a deadline to such notification, for example 15 days, i.e. if they have not received any message from the beneficiary within 15 days of the date of the amendment they could deem that it has been accepted by the beneficiary?

Analysis

Sub-Article 9(d)(iii) states that the beneficiary should give notification of acceptance or rejection of amendment(s). But it then goes on to state that if he fails to give such notification, the tender of documents to the nominated bank or issuing bank that conform to the credit and to not-yet-accepted amendment(s), will be deemed to be notification of acceptance by the beneficiary of such amendment(s), and, as of that moment, the credit will be amended.

ICC Position Paper No. 1 of 1 September 1994 states: "The Banking Commission strongly disagrees with the wrong practice adopted by:

a) certain Issuing Banks, of issuing irrevocable documentary credits, or amendments to irrevocable documentary credits, incorporating a provision to the effect that any amendment will become automatically effective unless formally rejected by the beneficiary within a specified period of time, or by a specified date;

b) certain Advising Banks, of adding a provision of the nature set out in (a) above when advising an irrevocable documentary credit, or an amendment to an irrevocable documentary credit.

The practices referred to above are seen as changing the irrevocable nature of the documentary credit irrevocable undertaking."

Conclusion

1) Yes.

2) This is against the principle of an irrevocable documentary credit as stated in UCP and ICC Position Paper No.1.

SUB-ARTICLE 14(d)   R 332

Does accepting discrepant documents mean that a bank has to accept similar discrepancies on future drawings?

Query

Documents that we had previously presented to an overseas bank were rejected due to the fact that an insurance certificate was presented in lieu of an insurance policy. This discrepancy was accepted by the applicant for the first two shipments.

We have now presented a third set of documents which contained the same discrepancy. The overseas bank has notified us that the applicant refuses to accept the documents on the basis of a certificate instead of a policy of insurance being presented.

We seek your expert advice as to whether this course of action is acceptable.

Analysis and conclusion

The fact that a bank may have previously accepted discrepant documents, with or without an applicant waiver, does not bind that bank to accepting a similar discrepancy(ies) on any future drawing(s) unless local law states otherwise.

SUB-ARTICLES 23(a)(ii) and 23(a)(v)   R 349

Whether the phrase "substitute vessel" constitutes a "similar qualification" under sub-Article 23(a)(ii)

Query

We would refer to Document 470.TA18 and request further comment on the basis of a bill of lading which we have accepted in our capacity as negotiating bank.

The bill of lading in question is worded, on its face, as follows: 'Received from the shipper in apparent good order and condition unless otherwise indicated herein, the goods or the container(s) or package(s) said to contain the cargo herein mentioned to be carried subject to all the terms and conditions provided for on the face and back of this bill of lading, by the vessel named herein or by any additional or substitute vessel or means of transport chosen at the ... '.

The bill of lading has a pre-printed box with the words 'Shipped on Board the Vessel' and a place for date and signature.

Questions:

1) Is the pre-printed wording 'Shipped on board the vessel' of the bill of lading, the 'pre-printed wording' of the first paragraph of sub-Article 23(a)(ii) of UCP 500? Can this be considered as 'notation on the bill of lading' of the second paragraph of the same Article?

2) Is the fine print showing the terms and conditions of the bill of lading to be considered as making the named vessel on the bill of lading as 'an intended vessel' although such wording is not present on the bill of lading?

3) If the fine print of the above makes the named vessel on the bill of lading as 'an intended vessel' and the pre-printed wording 'Shipped on board the vessel' an on board notation, then should the name of the vessel already stated under 'ocean vessel' on the top left hand of the bill of lading be somehow typed after the pre-printed wording 'Shipped on board the vessel' to make the bill of lading truly conforming to the condition of sub-Article 23 (a)(ii) third paragraph which states that if the bill of lading contains the indication 'intended vessel' the on board notation must include the name of the vessel?

The following are questions on the Opinion rendered under Document 470/TA18:

1) Does the reply say that the fine print such as the above on the bill of lading make the named vessel 'an intended vessel'?

2) Does it consider the pre-printed wording 'Shipped on board the vessel' an on board notation?

3) Does the reply say that because the fine print makes the named vessel 'an intended vessel' and the pre-printed wording 'an on board notation', the name of the vessel has to be somehow typed or written by the carrier after the pre-printed wording 'Shipped on board the vessel' to comply with sub-Article 23(a)(ii)?

The following are my own observations for your reference:

1) The fine print does not make the named vessel an 'intended vessel'.
2) The pre-printed wording on the bill of lading is not an 'on board notation'.
3) Therefore, in the present bill of lading, the name of the vessel does not have to be repeated after the 'Shipped on board the vessel' since it is already stated under 'ocean vessel' in the bill of lading.

Analysis and conclusion

Questions:
1) The pre-printed wording "Shipped on board the vessel" is not the reference to loading on board as mentioned within the context of sub-Article 23(a)(ii). This is merely the shipping company's style of inclusion of an on board notation as mentioned in the second paragraph of the above sub-Article. Reference in the sub-Article to "Loading on board or shipment on a named vessel may be indicated by pre-printed wording ..." occurs where the bill of lading states, for example, "Shipped in apparent good order and condition ..." instead of (and as in your case) "Received from the shipper in apparent good order ... ".

2) Sub-Article 23(a)(ii) states that: "If the bill of lading contains the indication 'intended vessel', or similar qualification in relation to the vessel, loading on board a named vessel must be evidenced by an on board notation on the bill of lading which, in addition to the date

on which the goods have been loaded on board, also includes the name of the vessel on which the goods have been loaded, even if they have been loaded on the vessel named as the 'intended vessel' ".

3) Sub-Article 23(a)(v) also states: " ... appears to contain all of the terms and conditions of carriage, or some of such terms and conditions by reference to a source or document other than the bill of lading (short form/blank back bill of lading); banks will not examine the contents of such terms and conditions ... ". Reference in sub-Article 23(a)(v) to terms and conditions relate to those terms of carriage stated on the bill of lading, usually on the reverse of the bill of lading. The reference to a possible "additional" vessel within your bill of lading did not appear within those terms and conditions, but within the general acceptance notice the carrier gives regarding the cargo and the terms of its delivery. Use of the words "by any additional (vessel)" is the equivalent of "intended vessel".

Where the pre-printed statement "Shipped on board the vessel" appears, this should also have incorporated the name of the actual vessel even if this is the same vessel which appears under the heading "ocean vessel".

Following extensive deliberations between the ICC Banking Commission and the ICC Commission on Maritime Transport, we are able to reply to the questions on Document 470/TA.18 as follows:

1) Yes, but in the context of the inclusion of "by an additional" in the pre-printed text. Use of the words "by any additional (vessel)" would be considered to be a similar qualification to intended vessel in the context of sub-Article 23(a)(ii).

2) Yes.

3) The ICC Commission on Maritime Transport has provided the following definition on how reference to "substitute vessel" or a "substitute clause" in the pre-printed wording on the face of a bill of lading is to be interpreted: "Without knowing the intention of the drafters of UCP 500, an 'intended vessel' equates a 'vessel to be nominated' or 'vessel to be named' clause. This means that at the time of entering into the contract of carriage no named vessel has been agreed upon. Thus, the carrier may at a late stage nominate the particular vessel with which he wishes to perform the contract of

carriage. While it is rare for the carrier to be left with the flexibility to single-handedly decide with which vessel he wishes to perform the contract of carriage after it has been entered into, such situations do occasionally occur in long term contracts.

"A substitution clause is something entirely different. In the absence of a specific agreement to the contrary, the carrier must perform the contract of carriage using the named vessel. Should the carrier, for some reason, not be able to perform the voyage with that vessel (for instance, because of a total loss), he is not entitled to replace it with another one. On the other hand, even if the charterers want the vessel replaced, the carrier is under no obligation to do so.

Because a vessel's individual characteristics are less important in the liner trade than in the 'freelance' seagoing trade, there has been a long-standing practice giving owners the right to substitute the vessel named in liner bills of lading with another vessel. However, it is important to note that if a named vessel has been agreed upon, then a right of substitution must have been expressly agreed upon if the carrier is going to perform with a vessel different from that named in the contract of carriage.

Where contracts of carriage provide a substitution clause, the clause will normally be considered an option in the carrier's favour, i.e. although the carrier has the right to substitute the vessel the charterers cannot force him to do so. However, if the carrier does substitute, he is under the obligation to perform the carriage with a vessel of similar type and characteristics as the originally named vessel.

Should the named vessel suffer a total loss, or be considered a constructive total loss, before the owner has exercised his right of substitution, the carrier has no right to perform with the substitute vessel. This is simply because the carrier, without a very specific agreement to the contrary, has no discretionary right to unilaterally decide whether or not a particular voyage is to be performed. If this were the case, the carrier might be inclined to take into account market conditions before considering whether or not to use his right to substitute. The legal position is, therefore, that either with or without substitution clauses there is only one vessel linked to the contract of carriage.

If the vessel is lost, so is the contract of carriage and thus the right for the carrier to substitute.

This points to the fact that the mere existence of a substitution clause does not involve the risk of banks that the 'intended vessel' does, as long as the right to substitute has not been exercised and as long as the vessel is clearly named in the bill of lading. The named vessel is therefore a firm choice vessel and any equation of a substitution clause with 'intended vessel' is unfounded."

In the light of this clarification, we would confirm that a bill of lading which in its pre-printed form uses the words "or substitute vessel" is not to be considered as a qualification similar to "intended vessel", in the context of sub-Article 23(a)(ii). This Opinion replaces that given in Document 470.TA.18 and Opinion No. R.283 appearing in ICC Publication No. 596.

However, due to the inconsistent approach adopted by various shipping lines to the use of phrases such as "substitute vessel" or the like, we are unable to give a definitive opinion that ALL bills of lading incorporating a substitution clause will be acceptable.

For the purposes of this and any future issue(s), a bill of lading using the words "or substitute vessel" or "or any substitute vessel" will not be considered discrepant under the conditions stated in sub-Article 23(a)(ii).

SUB-ARTICLES 20(b), ARTICLES 23 AND 26 AND THE ICC DECISION ON ORIGINAL DOCUMENTS   R 433

Where bill of lading and signatures thereon are produced by imaging technology and sent via the Internet, can they qualify as original documents under sub-Article 20(b)?

Query

The purpose of this query is to clarify whether sub-Article 20(b)(ii) applies in relationship to Company A's bills of lading. As background, Company A has used imaging technology to produce our bills of lading since 1996.

The bills of lading are distributed by direct printing and subsequently sent by courier to our customers; or, for approved customers, we send them via the Internet. The documents are identical whether they are printed internally or via the Web as the signature is imaged onto the document.

As we expand our bills of lading into other markets, some banks have raised the question as to whether or not the facsimile signature qualifies under sub-Article 20(b), which reads:

'b. Unless otherwise stipulated in the Credit, banks will also accept as an original document(s), a document(s) produced or appearing to have been produced:

i. ... by reprographic, automated or computerized systems; ii. ... as carbon copies, provided that it is marked as original and, where necessary, appears to be signed.

A document may be signed by handwriting, by facsimile signature, by perforated signature, by stamp, by symbol, or by any other mechanical or electronic method of authentication.'

It is my understanding that International Financial Services Association (IFSA, formerly known as USCIB) has previously supported the fact that Company A's bill of lading is in compliance with sub-Article 20(b) as stated above. Furthermore, we have issued in excess of 500,000 bills of lading in North America, signed with the facsimile signature since 1996. I believe the confusion lies in our ability to deliver the aforementioned bill of lading via the Internet, which may be incorrectly interpreted as an electronic document. Any opinion regarding this matter is appreciated.

Analysis and conclusion

The text of the query includes the wording of sub-Article 20(b) which is relevant to this issue. In addition, the content of the ICC Decision on Original Documents dated 12 July 1999 needs to be recognized.

In that Decision, Section 2, Determination of Originality, states: "Banks undertake to determine whether a document appears on its face to be an original document, as distinguished from a copy. Except as expressly required by a letter of credit (including an incorporated term such as UCP 500 sub-Articles 23(a)(iv) or 34b), banks do not undertake to determine whether an apparent original is the sole original. Banks rely on the apparent intent of the issuer of the document that it be treated as an original rather than a copy. In this regard, a person sending a telefax or making a photocopy on plain paper or pressing through carbon paper presumably intends to produce a copy. On the other hand, a person printing a document on plain paper from a text that that person created and electronically stored presumably intends to produce an original. Accordingly, documents bearing facsimile signatures or printed in their entirety (even including the issuer's letterhead and/or signature) from electronically stored text are presumably intended by the document issuer to be original and in practice are accepted by banks as original."

Section 3.3 of the Decision looks at documents which bear a facsimile signature and states: "Banks treat a facsimile signature as the equivalent of a hand signature. Accordingly, a document that appears to bear the document issuer's facsimile signature is also treated as an original document."

The issue of originality with regard to bills of lading is covered in the context that Articles 23 and 26, for example, require the presentation of a sole original bill of lading or multimodal transport document. Such documents either specify on their face that the document is original or within the printed text on the face that "in witness whereof X original bills of lading have been signed ... ", or similar wording.

The signature on the bill of lading is classified as being a facsimile one and as such is acceptable under the terms of sub-Article 20(b).

In the context of the printed wording which appears on the face of the bill of lading or multimodal transport document, "originality" can be established. The signature on the bill of lading is classified as being a facsimile one and as such is acceptable under the terms of sub-Article 20(b).

The document, issued as described above, would be acceptable under UCP 500.

SUB-ARTICLES 34(f)(ii), 34(e) AND 35(b)   R 458

Questions concerning whether insurance must be precisely 110% or whether it can be rounded up; if the credit is silent regarding the insurance coverage, must the insurance cover the entire voyage reflected in the transport document?

Query

A bank has made the following enquiries regarding international standard banking practice with regard to insurance requirements in a letter of credit subject to UCP500:

Questions:

1) If the credit is silent regarding the amount of insurance coverage required, and the invoice amount is USD 99.00 CIF or CIP, must the insurance be precisely 110% (i.e. USD 108.00) or may it be for a larger percentage? If a larger percentage is permitted, is there an upper limit?

2) If the credit stipulates "Insurance for 110% invoice value" and the invoice is USD 99.00, must the insurance coverage be precisely 110% (i.e. USD 108.00) or may it be rounded up to USD 110.00 (which is actually 111.1111%) for example? If it may not be rounded up by such a small percentage, why is 110% a minimum in number 1 above and why should this same 10 % addition not be permitted here?

3) If in question number 2 the amount may be rounded up, is there a percentage, for example 5% or 10%, which may be applied?

4) If the credit is silent regarding the insurance coverage (sub-Article 35(b)), must the insurance cover the entire voyage reflected in the transport document, or is it sufficient to evidence an effective date of coverage as in sub-Article 34(e)? – i.e. cover may be effective on the proper date but may only cover a portion of the voyage reflected in the transport document.

5) In sub-Article 34(f)(ii), what do the words "100% of the gross amount of the invoice" mean in practice? For example, do they mean an invoice reflecting a payment schedule for goods or an invoice reflecting pre-payments or other deductions?

Analysis

Sub-Article 34(e) reads: "Unless otherwise stipulated in the Credit, or unless it appears from the insurance document that the cover is effective at the latest from the date of loading on board or dispatch or taking in charge of the goods, banks will not accept an insurance document which bears a date of issuance later than the date of loading on board or dispatch or taking in charge as indicated in such transport document."

Sub-Article 34(f)(ii) reads: "Unless otherwise stipulated in the Credit, the minimum amount for which the insurance document must indicate the insurance cover to have been effected is the CIF (cost, insurance and freight (... "named port of destination")) or CIP (carriage and insurance paid to (... "named place of destination")) value of the goods, as the case may be, plus 10%, but only when the CIF or CIP value can be determined from the documents on their face. Otherwise, banks will accept as such minimum amount 110% of the amount for which payment, acceptance or negotiation is requested under the Credit, or 110% of the gross amount of the invoice, whichever is the greater."

Sub-Article 35(b) reads: "Failing specific stipulations in the Credit, banks will accept insurance documents as presented, without responsibility for any risks not being covered."

Conclusion

Question 1
Where the credit is silent as to the (minimum) amount of coverage, sub-Article 34(f)(ii) states the insurance document must be issued for a minimum of 110% of the CIF or CIP value. The UCP does not provide for any maximum percentage (ICC opinion under reference TA.111).

Question 2
The inclusion in an L/C of a term such as "Insurance for 110% invoice value" is a bank's way of trying to mirror the UCP requirement of 110%. However, it has not always been translated as such. Consistent with the UCP construction, banks that issue credits with such a clause are generally looking for a minimum coverage rather than an exact one. If a bank requires the insurance document to be issued for exactly

X% or X amount or words to similar effect, then the credit must expressly state this requirement. *This opinion overrides Issue 2 of query R195 which appears in ICC Publication No. 565.*

Question 3
Not applicable.

Question 4
Unless otherwise stipulated in the credit, the insurance document must cover the entire journey between the place from which the credit stipulates the goods are to be shipped or dispatched and the place to which the credit stipulates the goods are to shipped/delivered.

Question 5
100% of the gross amount of the invoice is the value of the goods before any deduction. For example, a credit which is issued for USD 100,000.00 and allows for 80% to be drawn against shipping documents with 20% having been paid in advance. This would entail the beneficiary producing an invoice for 100% of the goods value (USD 100,000.00) and showing a deduction in respect of the advance payment – resulting in a bottom line figure of USD 80,000.00

In this case, the insurance must be for a minimum of 110% of the gross amount of the goods (goods value USD 100,000.00 plus minimum 10%) and not a minimum of 110% of USD 80,000.00.

ICC AT A GLANCE

ICC is the world business organization. It is the only representative body that speaks with authority on behalf of enterprises from all sectors in every part of the world.

ICC's purpose is to promote an open international trade and investment system and the market economy worldwide. It makes rules that govern the conduct of business across borders. It provides essential services, foremost among them the ICC International Court of Arbitration, the world's leading institution of its kind.

Within a year of the creation of the United Nations, ICC was granted consultative status at the highest level with the UN and its specialized agencies. Today ICC is the preferred partner of international and regional organizations whenever decisions have to be made on global issues of importance to business.

Business leaders and experts drawn from ICC membership establish the business stance on broad issues of trade and investment policy as well as on vital technical or sectoral subjects. These include financial services, information technologies, telecommunications, marketing ethics, the environment, transportation, competition law and intellectual property, among others.

ICC was founded in 1919 by a handful of far-sighted business leaders. Today it groups thousands of member companies and associations from over 130 countries. National committees in all major capitals coordinate with their membership to address the concerns of the business community and to put across to their governments the business views formulated by ICC.

Some ICC Services
The ICC International Court of Arbitration (Paris)
The ICC International Centre for Expertise (Paris)
The ICC World Chambers Federation – (Paris)
The ICC Institute of World Business Law (Paris)
The ICC Centre for Maritime Co-operation (London)
ICC Commercial Crime Services (London), grouping:
The ICC Counterfeiting Intelligence Bureau
The ICC Commercial Crime Bureau
The ICC International Maritime Bureau

SELECTED ICC PUBLICATIONS

E: English – F: French – D: German – S: Spanish – EF: English/French bilingual edition – E-F: separate edition in each language

DOCUMENTARY CREDITS

Documentary Credit Law throughout the World

edited by Professor Rolf A. Schütze and Gabriele Fontane
Laws on documentary credits in more than 35 countries can be found in this essential compilation of letter of credit laws and practice. Written by two distinguished German lawyers, the book also contains a highly useful preface linking country statutes to the UCP, the ICC rules on letters of credit used by banks worldwide. Concise, practical and packed with useful information, this is an indispensable companion volume for all documentary credit professionals.

| E | 152 pages | ISBN 92.842.1298.7 | No. 633 |

DC Insight

International Trade Finance and Business Trends Quarterly
This ICC newsletter, published four times a year, keeps the reader updated on developments worldwide that impact directly on his or her business. ICC experts analyze how the UCP 500 is implemented in everyday situations, and there are national updates on documentary credit developments from correspondents in more than thirty countries. Along with hard-hitting interviews, all the latest L/C news, and regular supplements on electronic trends, you will also find he text of important court decisions concerning the UCP.

| E | Periodical/subscription | 4 issues a year |

Opinions of the ICC Banking Commission 1995–2001
Collected Queries and Responses

edited by Gary Collyer
Combining the past three published volumes with the latest Opinions, this hardback work includes a consolidated subject index as well as an index by Article, facilitating cross-referencing and checking. A mine of information that documentary credit practitioners will find a welcome addition to their reference bookshelf.

| E | 525 pages | ISBN 92.842.1297.9 | No. 632 |

Opinions of the ICC Banking Commission 1998–1999
Queries and responses on UCP 500, UCP 400 and URC 522

edited by Gary Collyer
The third volume in a series of ICC Banking Commission Opinions interpreting UCP 500, ICC's universally used rules on letters of credit. Containing more than 80 Opinions, this valuable reference work will serve as a guide to bankers, traders, practitioners and the courts as to how UCP 500 should be applied on a daily basis.

| E | 140 pages | ISBN 92.842.1268.5 | No. 613 |

More Queries and Responses on UCP 500 – Opinions of the ICC Banking Commission 1997
Over 50 queries, with a consolidated index.
E   92 pages   ISBN 92-842-1253-7   No. 596

ICC Guide to Documentary Credit Operations under UCP500
by Charles del Busto
With its unique combination of charts and sample documents, this guide illustrates the documentary credit process from the time of the credit application through the issuing process and concluding with the means of settlement. Using concrete examples of how documentary credits work in practice, with specific references to the UCP 500, this guide provides an indispensable tool for anyone involved in day-to-day credit operations.
E-F   112 pages   ISBN 92-842-1159-X   No. 515

Case Studies on Documentary Credits under UCP 500
by Charles del Busto
Analyzes in detail real-life cases involving the UCP 500. Taken from queries answered by ICC's Group of Experts, or structured from other cases submitted to ICC, *Case Studies* links the UCP Articles with factual explanations concerning their implementation. Each of the 33 case studies in this book is referenced to a specific Article of the UCP 500. In order to encourage individual training, the answers to the queries are grouped, case by case, in part two. A concrete and practical workbook to refer to time and again.
E   164 pages   ISBN 92-842-1183-2   No. 535

BANKING AND FINANCE

Bank Guarantees in International Trade
by R. Bertrams. *ICC Publishing/Kluwer Law International co-publication*
This fully revised second edition serves to broaden the understanding of bank guarantees, emphasizing the implications and issues which can arise in the daily functioning of these legal instruments. Written from a transnational perspective, the book has been updated and amended in the light of new developments in the law and changing patterns in practice, and accounts for the introduction of new techniques and problem areas.
E   450 pages   ISBN 92-842-1198-0   No. 547

A User's Handbook to the Uniform Rules for Demand Guarantees (URDG)
by Dr Georges Affaki
A clear and comprehensive guide that provides a masterly presentation of the rules within the context of day-to-day bank operations. The book covers the issuance, drafting, advantages and history of the rules and explodes a number of myths that have hindered more widespread adoption of the URDG. Complete with an index to the URDG Articles, as well as a general index, this practical handbook is destined to become the essential companion to all users of the URDG.

E   208 pages   ISBN 92-842-1294-4   No. 631

Bills of Exchange (third edition)
by Dr jur. Uwe Jahn
Now in its third edition, this fully revised publication has been expanded to cover legislation in Europe, Asia and Oceania. Designed for easy reference, the clear text provides a comprehensive comparison of bills of exchange law in 67 countries and offers practical information on everyday problems in overcoming conflicts in national laws. Dr Uwe Jahn is an acknowledged expert in the field and author of a number of books on international commercial law.

E   192 pages   ISBN 92-842-1250-2   No. 593

HOW TO OBTAIN ICC PUBLICATIONS

ICC Publications are available from ICC national committees or councils which exist in nearly 80 countries or from:

ICC PUBLISHING S.A.
38, Cours Albert 1er
75008 Paris – France
Customer Service:
Tel: +33 1 49 53 29 23/28 89
Fax: +33 1 49 53 29 02
e-mail: pub@iccwbo.org

ICC PUBLISHING, INC.
156 Fifth Avenue, Suite 417
New York, NY 10010
USA
Tel: +1 (212) 206 1150
Fax: +1 (212) 633 6025
e-mail: info@iccpub.net

To find out more about the latest ICC publications, visit our website at www.iccbooks.com